# Sociodrama

## *An Interpretive Theory for the Practice of Public Relations*

Thomas J. Mickey

University Press of America, Inc.
Lanham • New York • London

**Copyright © 1995 by**
**University Press of America,® Inc.**
4720 Boston Way
Lanham, Maryland 20706

3 Henrietta Street
London, WC2E 8LU England

**Library of Congress Cataloging-in-Publication Data**

Mickey, Thomas J.
Sociodrama : an interpretive theory for the practice of public relations
/ Thomas J. Mickey.
p.   cm.
1.  Public relations.  2.  Sociodrama.    I.  Title.
HM263.M456     1995        659.2--dc20        95-24032   CIP

ISBN 0-7618-0027-1 (cloth: alk ppr.)
ISBN 0-7618-0028-X (pbk: alk ppr.)

# Contents

# Preface

*A theory is a story with a plot whose ending is
satisfactory explanation, and whose main characters struggle heroically with obscurity for the
length of a hard journey through the territory of
difficulty and darkness, until the forest clears and
they emerge into the upland spaces of light and
clarity.*

— **Fred Inglis,** *Cultural Studies*

I once tried to sell an idea for a book dealing with several public
relations theories to various publishers. During fifteen years of teaching
public relations at the college level, I had collected a number of papers
and articles dealing with different public relations theories. I thought
that putting them together in one book would be helpful. Perhaps, one
day, that idea will see the light of print, but for the present it is important
that I discuss at least one alternative view of public relations.

This alternative view is called SOCIODRAMA, a theory that I have
been thinking about, writing about, and speaking about for a long time.
In addition to teaching public relations, I have been involved in public
relations practice for several years as a consultant. I have successfully
used the concept of sociodrama to help clients with their problems. What
I discuss in this project, therefore, is something that I have learned from
experience in the field of public relations and from my teaching of it.

If you are intimidated by the word "theory," remember that nothing
is more practical than a good theory (Kurt Lewin).

A theory is an attempt to explain something or understand it. A
discussion of any theory should include ideas, values, terminology, research methods, studies that corroborate the theory, and a list of authors
who recognize and support it. In regard to the latter, let it never be forgotten that no theory would ever be recognized if there were not some
devotees of that particular school of thought. Ideas are not necessarily
nor always logical. We like certain ideas and disregard others. We may
even have logical reasons for why we like or dismiss certain ideas. We
espouse certain ideas because they make sense to us. They make us feel
good about the way we look at the world. There is nothing inherently
wrong with that approach to ideas as long as we recognize it as such.

Publishers of books dealing with public relations seem to be looking for a reinforcement of one particular theory — a predominately pragmatic, positivist kind of theory rather than a cultural, humanist kind of theory.

When one looks at the field of public relations as a profession, one realizes that it is a practice as well as both a science and an art. At the same time, it constantly seems to be on the lookout for new techniques. Public relations professionals work to sway public opinion, advise management on strategic communication policies, promote something or someone, or continue favorable public opinion. These professionals are always looking for new and better ways to influence others.

What professionals may avoid in that search, however, is looking at public relations in a different way. If we view public relations as the influencing of others by providing a message that they will support, we have manifested a positivist approach to public relations. We can, for example, weigh our success by the amount of messages we put out in the print or broadcast media. Press clippings can be shown to a client or supervisor as an evaluation tool. It is not wrong to view public relations from that standpoint. It is, however, a narrow view of the public relations process. The public becomes something to be manipulated. Is any audience, be they internal or external (e.g. employees or consumers), that naive?

I was interested in looking at other ways to understand the public relations phenomenon, and what I present here is, hopefully, a coherent discussion of another view of public relations for the student, the public relations practitioner, the communications manager, and the public relations educator.

There is an order in presenting the theory. First, there must be a background. Second, we will discuss the meaning of sociodrama and how it ties in with public relations discourse. Third, we will look at some cases from this perspective. Finally, we will look at some strategies one might use in devising a plan that incorporates the sociodrama model. By the end of the book the reader will understand another way to look at public relations and know how to apply that theory to public relations practice.

What I hope will emerge from my work is a creative opportunity for both the student and the practitioner. Instead of merely memorizing the history, practices, and principles of public relations, as found in most texts today, perhaps we might see public relations being practiced with the insights from interpreting a public relations problem as sociodrama.

Sociodrama is truly an *interpretive* view of public relations.

I want to acknowledge my deep gratitude to the faculty of the School of Journalism and Mass Communication at the University of Iowa who first introduced me to many of these ideas.

I owe a thank you to my colleagues at Bridgewater State College, Bridgewater, Massachusetts for their continuing support and encouragement. I also want to recognize Bridgewater's Center for the Advancement of Research and Teaching (CART) for the grant I received which made it possible for me to finish this project.

The first person who put this entire manuscript into the computer was Kathy Sheehy. Without her help, this book would not have gotten off the ground. To Lynanne Clark, my typist, editor and graphics wizard, I am indebted for sticking with me during the many hours of what seemed like endless details.

Thanks to Rita Mae, who shows me in her smile every day that it is only love that matters.

TJM

# Chapter 1

# Thoughts on Public Relations and Public Relations Education

## Defining Public Relations: A Management Function

Public relations stands in need of a theory. That was the conclusion of Kulstad Van Slyke's research which suggested public relations should be viewed as a science (1980). A lot has happened in the field since that time. Unfortunately, Van Slyke's research links theory and science. One of the requirements for a science seems to be a well established body of theory that has been tested over a period of time. A **theory** of public relations, therefore, should be explored before venturing on to the question of whether to call public relations a science. Grunig (1993) points out that public relations researchers have made remarkable progress, and their work has reached the point where a general theory of public relations is in sight. Coleman and Durham (1993) tell us, however, that public relations remains epistemologically and theoretically underdeveloped. They looked at the public relations body of knowledge and concluded it was more a reflection of consensus-building than theory-building.

It is time to explore more theory-based approaches to the field of public relations.

Littlejohn lists the components of a theory as concepts, relationships, explanations, and value statements (1992). If one were to pick up any of the standard texts used in public relations courses around the country, one would find several different definitions of public relations but a consistent pattern throughout that is really one theory: a one-way, transmission view of public relations. Though concepts and explanations are offered, they highlight one kind of approach to the field (White, 1983). There are exceptions to a one-sided, positivistic view of public relations, such as the work of Grunig and Hunt (1986) and the Rybackis (1987). Botan and Hazelton also offer a look at other theories to use in public relations (1991).

Starck and Kruckenberg take a symbolic interactionist approach to the field (1990) in their look at community and public relations. The work of Heath and Toth proposes three different theories for the study of public relations: critical, systems, and rhetorical (1992).

There is a body of theory developing in the field of public relations. Marra (1993) proposes, for the first time, crisis public relations theory. Sriramesh (1993) studied the impact of culture on public relations practice, opening the door for a more cultural studies approach to the field. Obviously there is room for development in the field.

The popular definition of public relations, still remains: a "management function that seeks to understand public opinion and, using the organization's goals and objectives, creates a communication program to win favorable public opinion." (Wilcox, Ault, and Agee)

The key terms that turn up in the definition are "management function," "public opinion," and "communication program as action."

The term *management* refers to the source for effective public relations. Public relations is frequently ineffective unless the organization's chief manager or supervisor is directly involved. The top public relations professional in an organization should ideally be the Vice President or someone as close to that position as possible.

The emphasis on management in public relations has created a series of public relations texts (Wilcox, 1991; Nager and Allen, 1991). Their focus is that public relations ought to be considered a tool of management. Here public relations is seen as a means to achieve the goals of the organization. The public relations department does not come up with its own goals apart from those of the organization. In other words, the organization tells the public relations director what he/she is to achieve as the bottom line in his/her work.

The fallacy in the management component of the public relations definition is that all the decision-making seems to be done in one ball park. Though they may acknowledge the consumer, the employee, or the client, it is management that decides the course of action in dealing with them. The public interest seems to play a secondary role in the process. Olasky (1984) discusses this point in his critique of the prevailing paradigm of public relations. This prevailing paradigm approach is clearly one-sided and the side that controls it seems to be management. Such an approach needs to be questioned.

While it may be important to recognize public relations as linked to management, there are other questions that also need to be raised. Why deal with public relations as something that is one-sided? Does the public or audience who responds to management have any input in public relations decisions or output?

The traditional, positivist approach to public relations is one-sided, and does not take into consideration the human actors, both within and outside the organizations. It is therefore a somewhat misguided approach. In this field, we are dealing with human beings who think, feel, and interact through symbols (primarily language) in order to achieve their personal and common goals. It is time to construct a more humanistic approach to theory, one based on the humanities and not the model of an objective social science.

Where do we turn to get our grounding in the humanities approach? We turn to the fields of philosophy and literary criticism. MacCannell (1982) calls for a return to a liberal studies or interpretive approaches to studying human relationships. He says, "The interpretive and critical liberal arts have a better hand on the kinds of issues the world faces today than the positivistic sciences have."

The next term that is important in the discussion of public relations is *public opinion*. Public opinion is simply the way people view an organization, issue, product, or service. That view may either help or hinder an organization. Again, we see the link between public relations and the organization.

Negative public opinion can hurt an organization. It is the responsibility of any public relations director to prevent that from happening. At the same time it is the responsibility of the public relations professional to see that favorable public opinion continues.

There are public relations textbooks that teach the professional how to understand public opinion in order to promote favorable opinion and minimize negative opinion. There are a number of books like Nolte's (1979) that deal with gauging public opinion.

They seem, however, to look at public relations as manipulating behavior, or they see it as something that the organization *does* to win public support. The company manipulates the public along a certain line in order to convince the public to support the organization. Proponents of this theory believe that public opinion is a breeze that can switch direction at the whim of a talented and lucky practitioner. Olasky says,

"What current public discussion [of public relations theory] there is, goes on strictly within the boundaries of the current paradigm of manipulation. There is an awareness of anomalies, but they are not subjects of polite conversation."

The final key term in the definition of public relations is the *commu-*

*nication program.* There are several public relations texts that devote most of their discussion to researching and producing an effective public relations campaign. One example is the book by Cutlip and Center, which is a classic text for the field (1993). A new book on "Guerilla Public Relations" has just come on the market (Levine). The subtitle for the book is "How you can wage an effective publicity campaign — without going broke."

Cutlip and Center use the four-step process that has been adopted as the semi-official model of the Public Relations Society of America, the largest professional organization for public relations practitioners in the world. The four steps are research, planning, action, and evaluation.

If one looks at the reason for creating a communications program, it is again apparent that it is designed to do something *to* the audience that will get them to buy into the objectives of the management. It is often a program that is carried out for an ulterior motive — one which, for the most part, is summed up in the goals and objectives of the organization. A communication program, for example, may recommend press releases, features, videos, or special events to get people to do what you want.

This has been the traditional approach to public relations practice. Public relations education seems to follow that approach closely.

What underlies the understanding of and training in public relations work is a subtle brainwashing of the public. The classic book by public relations pioneer, Edward Bernays, is boldly entitled *The Engineering of Consent* (1955).

Bernays encourages those who wish to get involved in public relations to become acquainted with the behavioral sciences in an effort to understand how human beings interact. One eastern university, famous for its pioneering work in public relations education, refers to public relations as "applied behavioral science" (PRSA, 1994).

Underneath much of the current thought and curriculum of public relations education is a positivist approach that seems to dominate the field. This approach incorporates the belief that human success can be weighed by means of applied strategies. Facts — not inspirations, feelings, sentiment, or intuition — determine success.

Perhaps it is the nature of public relations that positivism is the only road for theory. Coleman and Durham certainly argue that case (1993). Perhaps, however, that road is simply the road that has received the most coverage. Certainly new graduates who approach their first jobs in public relations must practice the positivist approach if they are to succeed in the public relations field. Perhaps what is currently in print, however, is not the only way to understand or approach this field.

Historically it is important to know that since the 1940's public relations practice and education has relied almost exclusively on this positivist approach (Badaruco, 1990). We want to know how people will respond to the successful public relations campaigns we have created. We become successful public relations practitioners by applying the theory used in one campaign to another case. What worked in one time and place will surely work again.

In this process we imply a prediction and control model in public relations which is simply another facet of the positivist approach. Jerome Bruner, a psychologist, suggests there are other ways to look at human behavior (1983). We ought to do the same within the field of public relations. **The positivist approach is limiting when talking about human interaction. It is not the only way to look at human relationships or the practice of public relations.**

Most public relations textbooks explain that strategies in public relations are created in order to predict and control some form of human behavior. Public relations practitioners create a campaign that will change attitudes, give information, or create new behavior and convince others to support a certain cause or organization. Heath (1990) calls this the informational approach.

The true nature of public relations, however, does not call for a sole reliance on positivism. That approach is simply one that has worked and has received the most attention. As a result, what we know from books and articles written about public relations generally supports a theory closely aligned to positivism. The situation is quite different in the field of communication studies.

## Communication as a Field of Study: A Living Process

Perhaps public relations practitioners and public relations educators should use the field of communication as a model for understanding and teaching public relations. There are very different approaches to the study of human communication within the communications field. Two approaches one might take to the study of communication are *mechanistic* and *cultural*.

The mechanistic approach to communication can be found in books by Shannon and Weaver (1949), Carnegie (1983), and Hovland (1953). They imply that a result will take place because you set it in motion by some form of communication. There is a linear relationship between what you communicate and what you affect.

In Carnegie's work, for example, we see that the speaker's eye contact and smile are ways to effectively communicate with another person. As a salesperson, you will achieve rapport with your customer or client by using these techniques. There is a link between your action and the reaction of the other person.

Such an approach is called linear because there is a "line" between the communication behavior, such as a smile, and the response of the other person. The line goes from left to right, from the sender to the receiver (Shannon's term). One might diagram the mechanistic model in this way:

## FIGURE 1: Transmission Model of Communication

This is a popular way to discuss interpersonal communication in trendy psychology books like *The Well-Dressed Woman* (Drake, 1977), *Color Me Beautiful* (Jackson, 1987), *How to Make a Man Fall in Love With You* (Cabot, 1985), and *How to Work a Room* (RoAne, 1988).

These books imply that we communicate in a manner that creates a predetermined response in others. The key term here is ***predetermined***. We decide, by choosing how we communicate, what we want as a response: a smile, an acceptance, a word of welcome, a job, a partner.

Certainly other people are not *forced* to respond to us or our communication behavior, but these authors indirectly imply that there is not much choice on the part of the receiver. Our communication is effective when we have realized the desired response from the other person.

This approach is called "mechanistic" because it implies that we are like machines that can be turned on by some predetermined means. In this case, the means are the *right* communication behavior. This view does not leave room for, or seem to allow for, human initiative, free will, or the self determination of either the communicator or the other person.

This approach has been and continues to be quite useful to the communications manager. He/she must know what to expect if certain communication choices are made. For example, should I choose to send a memo to an employee or talk to the employee face to face? My communication behavior will have a different effect in each case.

The mechanistic view also recognizes that nonverbal communication behavior will impact the receiver. For example, a hospital worker dresses neatly for her work. At an interview for a different job at a high tech company, the interviewer asks her if she plans to dress as she is if she gets the new job. As you can guess, she is not offered the job. Her clothing has the effect of alienating her interviewer. Had she read one of the books on dressing for success, she would know that clothes *communicate* or *send a message* to others.

What value we might see in the mechanistic approach to the study of human communication is small compared to the vast amount of human experience it seems to exclude.

The second approach to the study of communication is the *cultural* approach. This theory looks at communication in a context called *culture*. Culture can be defined in the widest sense of the term to mean the way of life we create by the symbols we use every day. We have a family culture, a neighborhood culture, a city culture, and a national culture.

An essay by James Carey (1985) provides insight into the meaning and necessity of studying communication from this perspective. He argues that there is another way to look at communication and he calls it *cultural* or *ritual*. He says,

> The ritual view of communication has not been a dominant motif in American scholarship. Our thought and work have been glued to a transmission view of communication because this view is congenial with the underlying wellsprings of American culture, sources that feed into our scientific life as well as our common, public understandings. There is an irony in this. We understand that other people have culture in the anthropological sense and we regularly record it - often mischievously and patronizingly. But when we turn critical attention to American culture the concept dissolves into a residual category useful only when psychological and sociological data are exhausted... The notion of culture is not a hard-edged term of intellectual discourse for domestic purposes. This intellectual aversion to the idea of culture derives in part from our obsessive individualism, which makes psychological life the paramount reality; from our Puritanism, which leads to disdain for the significance of human activity that is not practical and work-oriented; and from our isolation of science from culture: science provides culture-free truth whereas culture provides ethnocentric error.

Delia and Grossberg defend an alternative approach, though their terms are *interpretive* and *scientific* (1977). Evans (1990) defends an interpretive turn in media research as well. What we have here, however, is the opposite view from the mechanistic.

MacCannell argues that the current alternative to a semiotics of culture and institutions is rationalism and positivism. By semiotics he simply means understanding the signs (symbols, primarily language) through which we interact in the culture, in our organizations, and in our relationships with one another.

This second approach to the study of human communication we might also call an INTERPRETIVE approach. This approach might, for example, discuss communication from a particular time frame such as the Industrial Revolution and the growth of the press. We understand the culture through its media technology, which embodies the values of the culture.

What this approach seems to imply in communication is that communication is understood in its historical context. We can make better sense of the form by seeing what setting it was in and what kind of culture the actors created.

For example, Kanter (1972) points out how American communes of the last century used communication forms to hold the group together. The language used and the clothes worn, for example, by different segments of the group indicated power or lack of it, and *became* the difference in their community culture.

In this model of communication, one communicator sees the other as valuable in himself rather than as someone to whom one can impart data or information. The emphasis is on the social order (i.e. family, friendship, marriage, city, culture) created by the interaction of communication. Davey (1993) studied photography as a way to understand how we create a world. Language incorporates the entire range of media and cultural artifacts through which we create and share meaning. We might also call this a *dramatic* view of communication. Carey says, "Under a ritual view (read cultural), news is not information but drama; it does not describe the world but portrays an arena of dramatic forces and action; it exists solely in historical time; and it invites our participation on the basis of our assuming, often vicariously, social roles within it."

Communication is a drama in which people assume roles within a certain social order. This drama is what we call a SOCIODRAMA. Sociodrama is closely linked to the cultural view of communication.

Public relations needs a theory that is *human* rather than mechanistic. It needs a theory that looks at human action as *action*, not motion or reaction. Such a view is the premise of this book — an interpretive theory based on public relations language. The theory is called SOCIODRAMA, a combination of both dramaturgical analysis and symbolic interactionism applied to the field of public relations.

A major source for the sociodrama view presented here is Hugh Duncan, who says, "We do not have selves and then form societies, but we form and develop a self in the give and take of what goes on between individuals within a society. (1985) Perenbanayagan (1985) echoes that thought when he says,"The objects of the world—man, world, space, time, and place included—are made available to human cognition, action, and interaction by a simultaneous process of naming, categorization, and or- dering by language."

We interact with one another through symbol. It is the symbol, mostly language, to which we give meaning. In the process we become part of a social order greater than ourselves (a family, a community, an organiza- tion). It is the cultural view of communication, or sociodrama, that puts emphasis on the symbols through which we not only understand our- selves, but we *become* ourselves.

Several philosophers, sociologists and historians have written exten- sively about symbols and communication. To support a cultural approach to communication study it might be helpful to quote a variety of authors who talk about symbol from this perspective.

Durkheim (1965) says, "Social life, in all its aspects and in every period of its history, is made possible only by a vast symbolism."

Cassirer (1962) says, "Instead of defining man as an 'animal ratio- nale' we should define him as 'animal symbolicum.'

When talking about self and symbol, Dillistone (1955) says, "Man only discovers his true self as he sets to work to organize his experience by the aid of symbols which carry a clear-cut meaning."

To know the symbols that we use is to know our culture. As Warner (1967) says,

> Sacred collective representations are symbol systems which for the mem- bers of the group express and refer to their collective life. They reflect and evoke what people feel and think themselves to be in times of social action. They symbolize what the values and beliefs of the group are. The group being a social and species system and such collective representa- tions symbolize for men what they feel and think about themselves as animals and persons.

Susanne Langer (1942) links symbols with the way we think in society when she says,

> Symbols are not proxy for their objects but are vehicles for the conception of objects. In talking about things, we have conceptions of them, not the things themselves; and it is the conceptions, not the things, that symbols directly 'mean.' Behavior toward conceptions is what words normally evoke; this is a typical process of thinking.

Finally, Hugh Duncan (1969) links symbols with the way we think in society when he says, "Symbolization must take forms which can become community or social dramas."

Symbols are not simply ways of expression, but *the* way of existence for us. We study a culture by its symbols. We know an organization by its symbols, especially language.

The interpretive approach to communication implies an acceptance of the meaning that the actors give to symbols as expressed through interaction. For that reason, the interpretive approach to communication assumes an on-going communication behavior that implies change in both the sender and the receiver in the communication process. This is much like the semiotics approach to culture (Portis-Winner) where we look at culture as signs structured to help us understand the system of which they are part, and vice versa.

Looking at the human person as a symbol-using animal means that as students of communication we are concerned with how people use and interpret symbols.

Symbols do not have their own inherent meaning. In interacting with others, we interpret the meaning of a symbol for ourselves and our needs. That aspect of the cultural view of communication and public relations is crucial: a cultural view means that the actors interpret symbols as they interact with one another.

Such a view seems to be quite different from the traditional positivist approach to communicating. We do not send messages to each other as an arrow flies through the air, rather, we interact with one another, interpreting the symbols each other uses in that interaction.

Hans Gadamer (1975) speaks of communication as an "hermeneutical" (interpreting) experience. He says,

> It is obvious that an instrumentalist theory of signs that sees words and concepts as handy tools has missed the point of the hermeneutical phenomenon...It must be emphasized that language has its true being only

in conversation, in the exercise of understanding between people. This is not to be understood as if that were the purpose of language. The process of communication is not mere action, a purposeful activity, a setting-up of signs, through which I transmit my will to others. Communication as such, rather, does not need any tools, in the real sense of the word. It is a living process in which a community of life is lived out...All forms of human community of life are forms of linguistic community: even more, they constitute language. For language, in its nature, is the language of conversation, but it acquires its reality only in the process of communicating. That is why it is not mere means of communication."

The interpretive approach to communication emphasizes the importance of understanding the actors' meanings for symbols they use in interacting with one another. We understand the culture by looking at how people interact with one another. The forms become part of the culture, which is experienced as interpreted by its actors or members.

Perinbanaygan says, "It is not that reality is theatrical or dramatic— rather what is considered reality by society, or a part thereof, is theatrically realized and constructed." One might sum up these two models by describing them in the words of Matson and Montague (1967):

> The field of communication is today more than ever a battleground contested by two opposing conceptual forces—those of monologue and dialogue. The 'monological' approach, which defines communication as essentially the transmission and reception of symbolic stimuli (messages or commands), finds its classical formulation in the art and science of rhetoric and its characteristic modern expressions in cybernetics, combative game theory, and the repertories of mass persuasion. The 'dialogical' approach, which regards communication as a path to communion, and the ground of self-discovery, found its original champion in Socrates and has its spokesman today in such diverse currents of thought as religious existentialism, post-Freudian psychotherapy, and sociological interactionism.

With the term *sociological interactionism*, we begin to see a different way to look at communication and public relations which have both been viewed too often from the positivist, mechanistic, or monological perspective.

# A Relationship between Public Relations and Communication

Is public relations the same as communication? Though they are not the same, one might argue for a link between the two, if only from a pedagogical viewpoint.

In many colleges and universities today public relations is taught in either a journalism department or a communication department. Recently there have been efforts to offer public relations degrees through business schools and departments (Ehling and Plank, 1987). There are not many public relations programs in schools of business today, although there may be a public relations course or two offered within other programs.

From the viewpoint of formal education in the field, therefore, there seems to be a strong link between communication, particularly mass media, and public relations. Hamilton and Terry (1987) point out that most public relations educators from the field of journalism see writing as the most important skill for a new practitioner entering the field. Writing still remains the primary entry-level skill for the profession of public relations.

Although there has been some criticism, the accrediting body for a college public relations sequence continues to be the Association for Education in Journalism and Mass Communication. PRSA has instituted its own accrediting process as well and a few institutions have sought it. It should be clear, therefore, that public relations education at the present time is strongly connected to communication study, especially education in the field of mass communication.

The question of the relationship between communication study and public relations study is important for two reasons. First, because certain assumptions can be made once we understand their relationship. Secondly, because we can broaden our study and practice of public relations by looking at it from the wider picture of communication study and practice.

Looking at the focus of formal education in public relations around the country, one could make two assumptions. First, we can assume that public relations is concerned with communicating to large numbers, particularly through the mass media. Second, we can say that writing is probably the most important skill for the public relations professional. One might rightly question these assumptions, but from the perspective of present public relations education we'd have to admit them.

Public relations is related to the study of communication in so far as planned communication is used to achieve the goal of the organization. We might say that public relations is applied communication, or communication that is used to move the organization's members or audience in a certain direction.

The issues that were raised earlier about the formal study of both public relations and communication are important issues to consider. Both the study of public relations and the study of communication have been burdened with a heavy emphasis on a one-sided approach: positivist, mechanistic, one-way, and monological. They therefore both suffer from some of the same problems indicative of a rather narrow body of theory. Communication authors have had more success in arguing for an interpretive approach to communication study. In the case of public relations, however, scholars such as Wilcox (1993) seem to continue to link public relations with a more mechanistic, one-sided approach to communication. That approach needs to be balanced by an effort to study public relations in a more cultural context.

If we can study *communication* from a cultural perspective, why can't we study *public relations* from the same viewpoint?

By understanding the link between the two fields of study, we can broaden our understanding of public relations and go beyond simply sending a message from the organization to its various audiences in order to achieve the goals of the organization. We could look at it from a more cultural, dialogical definition.

We should realize that in public relations we can not merely send our audience a message and expect to it to manipulate them or their actions. Instead, we must understand that the audience participates in a drama in which we and they play roles. The public relations staff and the organization's target audience both identify with the organization and create a certain *culture* or way of life known and expressed in the symbols within that organization. The organization does not just send the public a message. Both parties interact with one another through a symbolic process, primarily the use of language. Such preliminary ideas are a preview of the interpretive approach to the study of public relations called sociodrama. It is quite different from the one-way approach mentioned earlier.

What is it that public relations people do? They *communicate* the message of the client to a target group. That target group may be an internal audience like employees or an external audience like customers. The public relations professional must study, informally if not formally, the theories and principles of effective communication. That study should not concentrate on a one-way or manipulative form of communication, but should focus on theories of communication which include both positivist and cultural approaches.

Someone who has been practicing public relations for a number of years may be working under one theory of what constitutes public relations practice. He/she uses that theory in developing projects. There is nothing wrong with that, except that it may become quite limiting in the course of one's career. It is the job of a public relations researcher to come up with alternatives to the current views within the field, much the way a lab scientist works to come up with new theories to explain a scientific phenomemon to other scientists who cannot spare the time to explore it themselves. It becomes the responsibility, however, of those not conducting research to stay tuned in to new developments in the field. It could be the same within the field of public relations. For growth and development to occur within any field, new research  must be admitted and recognized by those practicing as well as those educating.

Another term for public relations is communication management, or managing communication to promote the goals and objectives of the organization. The term indicates a connection between creating effective communication strategies and carrying them out.  The public relations professional within the organization manages various communication strategies to affect change in order to promote the goals of the organization.

For example, a personnel department in a hospital is charged with making the employees aware of the new insurance policies.  The public relations department sees to it that employees get that message.

How do they begin? The personnel and public relations departments will meet and create a public relations plan or strategy.  In that strategy they might list the objectives, media options, messages, budget, and timing that serve the organization most effectively.  They might decide to use meetings, the newsletter, bulletin boards, circulars, mailings, or another form of communication.  They can effect change, which could be awareness and acceptance, by good use of communication strategy and activity.

So far we have seen two terms linking public relations to communication: *applied communication* and *communication management.*

Note that in using both terms we talk about *communication* as the one which defines public relations.  For the sake of discussion, it is important to understand this emphasis on communication.  It is important that the student, practitioner, and educator widen his understanding of the term *public relations* to include the central issue of communication. And, just as the field of communication has several approaches within it, it makes sense that the field of public relations might profit from considering a new perspective, sociodrama.

# References

Badaracco, C. (1990). Publicity and Modern Influence. *Public Relations Review*, Vol. 16, 3, Fall, pp. 5-18.

Bernays, E. (1955). *The engineering of consent*. Norman: University of Oklahoma Press.

Botan, et al Ed. (1989). *Public Relations Theory*. Hillsdale, N.J: Lawrence Erlbaum, Associates.

Bruner, J.S. (1983). *In search of mind: Essays in autobiography*. New York: Harper Row.

Cabot, T. (1984). *How to make a man fall in love with you*. New York: St. Martin's Press.

Cabot, T. (1985). *How to make a man fall in love with you*. New York: Dell

Carey, J. (1989). *Communication as Culture*. Boston: Unwin Hyman

Carnegie, D. (1983). *How to win friends and influence people*. New York: Simon & Schuster.

Cassirer, E. (1962). *An essay on man: An introduction to a philosophy of human culture*. New Haven: Yale University Press.

Coleman, C. & Durham, F.D. (1993). *Articulating paradigm and body of knowledge within public relations*. Paper presented at the International Communication Association. Washington, D.C.

Cutlip, S., Center, A.H., & Broom, G.M. (1994). *Effective public relations* (7th ed.). Englewood Cliffs, N.J. Prentice Hall.

Davey, G.J. (1993). *Understanding Photographic Representation: Method and Meaning in the Interpretation of Photographs*. Dissertation abstracts. University of Iowa.

Delia J.G., & Grossberg, L. (1977). Interpretation and evidence. *Western journal of speech communication,* 41, 32-42.

Dillstone, F.W. (1955). *Christianity and symbolism*. London: Collins.

Drake Hemingway, P. (1977). *The Well-Dressed Woman*. New York: Signet Books.

Duncan, H. (1969). *Symbols and social theory*. New York: Oxford University Press.

Duncan, H. (1985) *Communication and social order.* New Brunswick, U.S.A.: Transaction Books.

Durkheim, E. (1965). *The elementary forms of the religious life*. New York: Free Press.

Edelman, M. (1988). *Constructing the Political Spectacle*. Chicago: University of Chicago Press.

Ehling, W. P. and Plank, B. (1987). *The Design for Undergraduate Public Relations Education*. New York: Public Relations Society of America.

Evans. (June 1990). The interpretive truth in media research: Innovation/ Iteration/Illusion. *Critical Studies in Mass Communication.* 7, 147-168.

Gadamer, H.G. (1975). *Truth and method.* London: Sheed & Ward.

Grunig, J., & Hunt, T. (1984). *Managing public relations.* New York: Holt,Rinehart & Winston.

Grunig, J., & Hunt, T. (1986). *Application of open systems theory to public relations: Review of a program of research.* Paper presented to the International Communication Association, Chicago.

Hamilton, P., & Terry, K.E. (1987). *A comparative analysis of public relations programs.* Paper presented to the Speech Communication Association, Boston.

Hovland., C.I., Janis, I.L., & Kelley, H.H. (1953). *Communication and persuasion: Psychological studies of opinion change.* New Haven, CT: Yale University Press.

Jackson, C. (1987). *Color Me Beautiful.* New York: Ballantine.

Kanter, R.M. (1972). *Commitment and community: Communes and utopias in sociological perspective.* Cambridge, MA. Harvard University Press.

Kulstad van Slyke, J. (1980). *Defining public relations: Toward a theory of science.* Paper presented to the Association for Education in Journalism and Mass Communication, Boston.

Kruckeberg, D. & Starck, K. (1988). *Public relations and community: A reconstructed theory.* New York: Praeger.

Langer, S.K. (1942). *Philosophy in a new key: A study in the symbolism of reason, rite and art.* New York: Mentor Books.

Levine, M. (1993). *Guerrilla P.R.: How you can wage an effective publicity campaign — without going broke.* New York: Harper Business.

Littlejohn, S.W. (1993). *Theories of human communication,* (4th Ed.). Belmont, CA: Wadsworth Publishing.

MacCannell, D., & MacCannell, J.F. (1982). *The time of the sign: Semiotic interpretation of modern culture.* Bloomington: Indiana University Press.

Marra, F. J. (1993). *Crisis Public Relations: A Theoretical Model.* Dissertation abstracts, University of Maryland College Park.

Matson, F.W., & Montagu, A. (Eds.). (1967). *The human dialogue: Perspectives on communication.* New York: The Free Press.

Nager, N. and Allen, T. H. (1991). *Public relations management by objectives.* Lanham, MD: University Press of America.

Nolte, L.W. (1979). *Fundamentals of public relations: Professional guidelines, concepts and integration.* New York: Pergamon Press.

Olasky, M. (1984). *The Aborted Debate within Public Relations: An Approach through Kuhn's Paradigm.* Paper presented to the Association for Education in Journalism and Mass Communication.

Perinbanayagam, R.S. (1985). *Signifying acts: Structure and meaning in everyday life.* Illinois University Press.

Perinbanayagam, R.S. (1991). *Discursive Acts.* New York: Aldine de Gruyter.

Portis-Winner, I. (1988). Research in semiotics of culture. In Thomas A. Sebeok & Jean Umiker-Sebeok. (eds.) *In The Semiotic Web 1987.* (pp. 601-636). Berlin: Mouten de Gruyter.

RoAne, S. (1988). *How to work a room: A guide to successfully managing the mingling.* New York: Shapolsky Publishers.

Rybacki, K., & Rybacki, D. (1987). *Public rhetoric and public relations.* Paper presented to the Speech Communication Association, Boston.

Shannon, C.E., & Weaver, W. (1949). *The mathematical theory of communication.* Urbana, Il: University of Illinois Press.

Sriramesh, K. (1992). *The Impact of Societal Culture on Public Relations: An Ethnographic Study of South Indian Organization* (India). Dissertation abstracts. University of Maryland College Park.

Toth, E., & Heath, R.L. (1992). (Ed.). *Rhetorical and critical approaches to public relations.* Hillsdale, N.J: Lawrence Erlbaum Associates.

Warner, W. L. (1961 ) . *The family of God: A symbolic study of Christian life in America.* New Haven, CT: Yale University Press.

White, R.A. (1983). *Mass communication and culture: Transition to a new paradigm.* Journal of Communication, 33 (3), 279-301 .

Wilcox, D.L., et al. (1990). *Public relations: Strategies and tactics.* New York: Harper Collins College

Yarrington, R. (1983). *Community relations handbook.* New York: Longman.

# Chapter 2

# Messages and Drama

## Introduction

The explanation of sociodrama in this chapter will include its origin, principle concepts, its focus on language, and its usefulness in understanding human behavior. Then a discussion of the ten primary axioms of sociodrama will be discussed to give flesh to the theory. What will become clear through this discussion is that the theory of sociodrama relies on the major schools of thought referred to as *dramatism* (also called dramaturgy) and *symbolic interactionism*.

Any discussion of sociodrama must spend a significant amount of time on the author who here is the primary source of the concept: Hugh Dalziel Duncan (1909-1970). Primarily a communication writer, Duncan's ideas can enlighten the field of public relations.

Born in Scotland in 1909, Duncan was a trained sociologist but was considered persona non grata in the field of sociology because of his refusal to follow the strict "scientific" approach to research in his field. Defending his position, he once said, "There is no proper 'way' to be scientific, and even if there is a proper way in physics, it does not follow that this is the way to be scientific in sociology." He opposed the scientific method of social science in which prediction and control were the objectives. His approach was one of *understanding*. From his work, one can see that Duncan was more interested in a *cultural* study of communication than in the *transmission* view of communication.

He found in the field of literature a preferable way to study the human condition. He combined his interest in language with his attempts to understand how society works. For Duncan literary criticism became the means to understand how society evolves.

Duncan was struck by the *drama* of human relationships. People are not born with relationships already in place. They create those relationships through form or symbol. Duncan sought to explain how people use words to interact with one another. He spent his life trying to construct a *dramatistic* image of social interaction. "Art," he said, "like any basic social institution, *constitutes* social relations, because it creates the forms in which these relationships take place."

At the time of his death, Duncan was Professor of Sociology and English at Southern Illinois University. Although he published several articles and books on the sociological aspects of communication, his most famous is *Communication and Social Order.*

The tradition of dramatism continues today with books by Young (1990) and Brissett and Edgley (1990). Goffman (1965) is certainly a pioneer in the field and cannot be ignored. Perinbanaygam (1985) combines the symbolic interactionist tradition with dramatism in his work, and expresses a new interest in exploring connections between dramaturgy, deconstruction, semiotics, feminist theory, and postmodernism.

## Sociodrama in Context:  Theories of Society

Burrell and Morgan (1979) have pointed out the important traditions of sociology as a social science  These are important traditions for understanding communication as well as public relations theory.

The two main views Burrell and Morgan discuss are "objective/subjective orientation" and the "sociologies of regulation/radical change." [See Figure 2, next page]

Two of the four areas in the matrix are radical humanism and interpretive sociology which are closer to the "subjective" pole.  The other two areas are radical structuralism and functionalist sociology which are closer to the "objective" pole.

The important contribution that Burrell and Morgan have made is that the various schools of sociological thought can be situated in a tradition and in relation to other ways of studying society.

According to Rosengren (1983), most communication research has been located in the lower right-hand objective cell of "functionalist sociology."  Research of this type is heavily criticized by the other "dissident" schools of thought which reside primarily in the left-hand boxes of the diagram.

The lower left-hand box is highlighted by the concern for questions of both "subjective" and "interpretive sociology." The schools of thought in both theory and research that take these paths are phenomenology, hermeneutics, and phenomenological sociology. This is where discourse analysis and semiotics, which have a special significance for sociodrama, might find a spot as well.

Though the Burrell and Morgan typology mirrors the situation in sociology in the late 1970's, many of the same schools and groupings appear today in communication research, albeit sometimes under different names. Rosengren (1993) says the big difference is that the relative importance of the two dimensions in the typology has shifted. In the late 1970's, the regulation/radical change dimension was predominant. Today, the subjectivistic/objectivistic dimensions have the upper hand in the humanities and the social sciences, as well as within communication. Sociodrama, in both theory and method, is more closely aligned with the lower left-hand area of the typology. Therefore, the major concern lies with interpretation and subjective meanings that people have in regard to something, and in this case, an organization. In sociodrama, public relations is viewed as subjective behavior.

Hellweg (1989) says that research in organizational communication is increasingly moving toward an interpretive perspective and away from a functionalist view.

Most public relations theory and research to date has been centered in schools of thought within the lower right-hand box: objective and functionalist. In comparison, sociodrama takes an interactive and interpretive approach. This is the approach to media study discussed by Carragee (1990). He says,

> Interpretive approaches to the study of mass communication behavior, which are described by their proponents as an alternative to 'deterministic' perspectives on media effects and media audiences, examine the intrepretive processes employed by audience members in their decoding of media texts, the social uses of these texts, and the social settings that shape media consumption. Accusing past research of ignoring audience activity, those who hold these perspectives view meaning as a product of the interaction between media texts and the multiple, at times, contradictory, interpretive strategies employed by audience members.

And in speaking of the methods within this interpretive approach, he says, "Ethnographic methods employed in interpretive mass communication research — detailed observation, depth interviewing, and the reliance on informants—are used extensively by interpretive sociologists and cultural anthropologists."

But he is not without an important criticism of the interpretive approach as a response to the positivist method of research: "Interpretive approaches suggest that mass communciation [here also public relations research] has failed to examine the purposive activity of social actors who are engaged in media (or public relations) use."

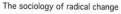

Figure 2: Burrell and Morgan Typology

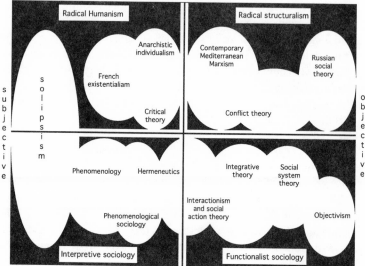

A criticism of the interpretive approach is that not enough emphasis is given to the context in which the subject creates meaning and the context in which the text is produced. We hope to address these issues in building the case of a sociodrama for public relations in which we emphasize the symbol and the subject. Carragee argues that interpretive researchers need to devote far more attention to the properties and structures of communication messages, i.e., to the symbolic power of texts.

Heath (1993) calls for a rhetorical theory of public relations in which the quest for the subjective meanings that people have about organizations and their relationships with them is important. Meaning is created and expressed through discourse. Heath proposes a rhetorical paradigm rather than an information paradigm — which is asymmetrical or one-sided, i.e. passing information from the organization to the public or stakeholder. Sociodrama concerns itself with the language of pubic relations and is interactional, interpretive, and cultural. Therefore, one might argue that the sociodrama perspective is more aligned with Heath's rhetorical approach to the field of public relations.

## Sources for Duncan

The MacCannells' (1982) work on signs and symbols in society argues for consideration of symbol and drama in everyday life as if they themselves were students of Duncan:

> Even everyday life proliferates cultural productions that serve as metasystems of interpretation: from below the level of the individual to the self and beyond, to class, and to any human system, we engage in a *drama* of interpretations that is the mechanism (secondary modeling systems) of cultural development. (p.26)

The sources of Duncan's ideas about sociology come primarily from the school of symbolic interactionism at the University of Chicago. In the history of communication study, the Chicago School is one of the major birthplaces for the development of the field. Though a school of sociology, the scholars here placed communication at the center of their conception of human behavior (Rogers, 1994). There Duncan studied George Herbert Mead, John Dewey, Charles Horton Cooley, Robert E. Park, Edward Sapir, and Benjamin Whorf. Duncan's view of literature and the role of the critic, however, came from another source — Kenneth Burke.

Duncan studied the question of how we use language as a way to justify, explain, motivate, and understand each other. He approached the study of society through the use of forms, especially language, in our interactions with one another.

Duncan seems to write for the public relations practitioner when he says:

> The rise to power of the publicist (the modern Sophist) indicates that, as differentiation increases in large corporate structures, consensus will depend more on our ability to think about communication as symbolic action...In solving the problem of how to establish favorable conditions for appeals to customers, American businesses, working in a free economy, have not been able to rely on monopolies of symbols (as in a priestly caste), of technical means of communication (as in a dictatorship), or of training in communicative skills (as in clerical orders). He has been forced to develop skills in persuasive techniques, always in competition with other businessmen as well as with other agencies or institutions in the state.

Kuhn (1964) attributes the beginning of the social theory called symbolic interactionism to the oral tradition of James, Cooley, Dewey, and Mead that preceded the 1937 publication of Mead's *Mind, Self, and Society*. Mead's publication, however, was the important turning point in the history of this American school of social thought.

Through the years, the theory of symbolic interactionism has been used to study human behavior in such diverse fields as family therapy, community development, religion, and advertising. Symbolic interactionism asserts that a person carves out his social existence. He/she does not merely conform to group norms. Cultural norms, status positions, and role relationships are only the framework within which social action takes place and not the crucial and coercive determinants of that action. Symbolic interactionism perceives the human being as creating or remaking his/her environment with a course of action, rather than simply responding to normative expectations.

Concerning the question of communication, therefore, symbolic interactionists would say that we *interact* in communication. The participants or actors construct a relationship, or destroy it, through symbols of communication. Duncan was concerned with the relationship among symbol, communication, and social order. He focuses on this concern in his model called "sociodrama" and leans heavily on Kenneth Burke's discussion of dramatism.

Burke (1962) wrote about dramatism in the *International Encyclopedia of the Social Sciences*. This article, which summarizes his thoughts, came at the twilight of Burke's voluminous career as a writer which spanned almost 50 years. Reukert (1963), a critic and student of Burke, helps us understand him. He says of Burke:

> For many people Burke exists in fragments, as the originator of a few stunning ideas and the writer of sporadically brilliant applied criticism. And yet his power comes from, and his real achievement consists in, the monolithic dramatistic system he has developed. Everything since the early forties has been written from within that system, and is either an application or an extension of it.

Burke's work can be summarized in his dramatistic view of the human person. For Burke, the person in search of himself and a better life is the universal situation, and the complex drama of this situation is a major part of all his work.

Dramatism is the essence of Burke's work. He says that dramatism is "a method of analysis and a corresponding critique of terminology designed to show that the most direct route to the study of human relations and human motives is via a methodological inquiry into cycles or clusters of *terms and their functions*." (1968)

Note Burke's reference to "terms." He stresses the importance of looking at the language we use to understand how we relate. It is the term we use that creates the relationship.

Mangham and Overington (1990) say:

> For Burke and for ourselves, working and writing in a dramatistic key, people are actors who play characters; they are works of dramatic art...It is through language that we become self-conscious, capable of playing a number of characters to varying audiences and yet still retaining a grasp of an acting self. In this notion of the distinction between ourselves and our roles — a theatrical consciousness, if you will — exist the links between dramatism and the tradition of symbolic interactionism that stretches from the work of James, Cooley, and Mead to the present.

Davis discussed the importance of "symbolic" to the symbolic interactionist tradition, which is something that tradition seems to have forgotten. Evidently symbolic interactionists have not taken the issue of symbol seriously because it is discussed again ten years later. This time Boden (1990) makes the point that rarely are language and meaning objects of symbolic interactionist inquiry; rather they typically serve as resources out of which the essentially shared and social nature of society is conjured.

As a method, dramatism addresses the empirical questions of how persons explain their actions to themselves and others, and what the cultural and structural influences of these explanations might be. Burke's concern in dramatism is the persuasive or rhetorical link between motivation and action. Language is seen as social action. Language is not simply a way to express oneself, but a way to relate to both self and others. That self is as rhetorically defended as it is rhetorically constructed is the key to sociodrama (Perinbanayangan, 1985).

Unlike most positivistic social science, dramaturgical thinking is not a linear, sequential explanation of human behavior based on mechanistic assumptions. Its point of departure is Kenneth Burke's profound assertion that the difference between a thing and a person is that a thing merely moves whereas a person *acts*. The language of mechanism is therefore inapplicable to the study of human selves. (Burke, 1966, p. 53)

As a result, sociodrama might also be called a "rhetorical" approach to public relations. The paradigm that is most likely to generate the preferred research and strategies in public relations practice is rhetorical rather than informational (Heath, 1993).

The ancient and honorable art of rhetoric is the art of persuasion about which public relations is most concerned. Along with grammar and logic, rhetoric has held an important place in education for almost twenty five centuries. Its status was much more important in Greek and Roman antiquity, when an educated person was expected to be something of an orator. It was also held in high regard in the seventeenth and eighteenth centuries, when the emphasis in speech and writing was on style as well as substance.

Those investigators (Burke, 1968; Duncan, 1968; Perinbanayagam, 1985) who are bent on establishing the legitimacy of dramatism or dramaturgy as a distinctive form of social thought subscribe to the view that life is **drama**. For them, dramaturgical understanding is that long-sought, clear window into human reality. Perinbanayagam (1985), whose recent work provides us with the most careful and detailed examination of the dramaturgical position to date, argues most forcefully for the idea of drama as reality.

Drama as an ontology begins with the premise that humans cannot help but communicate with symbols, and cannot help but be aware that others around them are interpreting those symbols. Such communication is achieved with selected features of communication media. The world consists of communication-worthy social facts or social objects that dramatically develop and present a theme. The theater is not something apart from society, or something that society invented — it is a crystallization and typification of what goes on in society all the time, or more sharply, what a social relationship is (Perenbanayagam, 1985).

## Axioms

The theory of sociodrama as explained in this text has certain truisms, or axioms, that can be used to both understand the theory and apply the theory to practice. Within the sociodrama theory one might propose ten such axioms.

---

### Axiom #1
*Language is a way of explaining and a way of creating motives that lead to a certain kind of action.*

---

This axiom suggests a clear link with public relations. It is the language used that enables the participants (e.g., the company's public relations professional and the company's publics) to act in a certain way.

Dramatism emphasizes three key words: language, motives, and action. Dramatism is a systematic approach to understanding human action through an analysis of the motives — the explanations — that people offer as accounting devices for such action. Note the word "accounting." How we talk and write about ourselves, our work, and our organization both motivates and explains the action we perform.

Symbolic interactionism and dramatism, therefore, are linked and form the basis of sociodrama. Sociodrama obviously relies heavily on the interpretive/subjective view of society: The human world is an interpretive experience. The world does not reveal itself. We formulate it as interpretable through language and other symbols.

Language is the way roles are created in an effort to relate to one another, whether in a family or in a business. Unless we talk and write, we can not understand ourselves or our relationships. Without language we cannot act toward each other. It is Duncan who brought the two schools of symbolic interactionism and dramatism together in what he called sociodrama.

Blyler (1992) studied the role of rhetoric in understanding public relations writing. She found that narratives were particularly important because they provided a comprehensive, compelling framework for belief and thus contributed greatly to the shared meaning created by writers and readers.

There have been studies that explore how people become who they are through words spoken and written about them. Gitlin (1980) describes the creation of an organization by the news media called Students for a Democratic Society (SDS). He looked at the Times and CBS news footage from what is called the literary-linguistic analysis perspective, an in-depth look at what is written and spoken. He noted how the writer used position, placing, treatment, tone, and stylistic intensification, all of which formed an imagery that journalists used in their stories. The SDS members found themselves trying to live up to an image of them that was portrayed in the media. The heroes and villains *became* the way they were treated in the media.

Gitlin's work was not simply a study of the *content* of material produced by the New Left media to demonstrate distortion. Gitlin studied the political significance of the material and revealed the politics of media institutions as well as the influence of the media upon the organization. At one point Gitlin explains that new SDS members became disillusioned with the organization when what they experienced did not measure up to what they saw on TV or read in the papers.

Goodman (1978) sees science, art, and other cultural forms as "ways of worldmaking" through symbol. Edelman (1988) says the most incisive twentieth century students of language, although working from different premises, collectively conclude that language is the primary creator of the social worlds people identify with, not a tool for describing an objective reality.

---

**Axiom #2**

*Sociodrama is not concerned with only content or agency in communication but how people use the words to define themselves.*

---

In a research project on the subject of alcohol consumption, Gusfield (1976) describes how the social scientist acts as a dramatist—setting a stage and persuading his readers to treat his work as one type of production rather than another. He argues that if words, sentences, paragraphs, and larger units are a major tool for reporting and persuading, an analysis of how scientific knowledge leads to practical action cannot ignore the language and literary style of the field of science.

In writing about social and problem drinkers, Gusfield shows the influence in the practice of writing. He specifically relates how a scientific report about the problem-drinker not only explains but *creates* the type of drinker that needs help. In the act of developing and presenting particular data, the theorizing and/or conclusion-making stems from acts of selection, nomenclature, artistic presentation, and language. To be relevant or significant, data must not only be selected, but must also be typified and interpreted. In doing this, language and thought are themselves the vehicles through which such relevance is cast. In Burke's terms they are "modes of action."

By writing and reading about problem drinkers, those in the helping profession recognize them in their work and recommend appropriate treatment. In classifying them as "the clients," the role of counselor is assumed. The language becomes the way to relate, not simply the means to talk about the problem.

Goffman (1974) discusses everyday conversation as sociodrama when he says:

I am suggesting that often what talkers undertake to do is not to provide information to a recipient but to present dramas to an audience. Indeed, it seems that we spend most of our time not engaged in giving information but in giving shows. And observe, this theatricality is not based on mere display of feelings or faked exhibitions of spontaneity or anything else by way of the huffing and puffing we might derogate by calling theatrical. The parallel between stage and conversation is much, much deeper than that. The point is that ordinarily when an individual says something, he is not saying it as a bald statement of fact on his own behalf. He is recounting. He is running through a strip of already determined events for the engagements of his listeners.

Goffman implies that we speak in dramatic metaphor as a primary way of engaging our listeners. We add our own *interpretation* in the process in order to portray the consummate actor— one who has an audience. Indeed, our dialogue then becomes the way to link with one another.

Preaching as sociodrama becomes a way of forming a parish and justifying certain kinds of social behavior (Mickey). Sermons are used by the parish as ways of establishing motives for greater or lesser involvement in issues like abortion or nuclear energy. The actors, preacher and congregation, construct the kind of parish they want in and through the sermon. The sermon therefore is not just a vehicle to expound religious dogma, but through word selection, intonation, theme, and framing, is a way for both preacher and congregation to construct a particular kind of social reality. People say they go to a particular church because they "like" the sermons. The words persuade them to be part of the church and indeed *are* their link with the church. They find themselves by identifying with the sermon. They become "religious" because of the language used. How often do we hear people say it is their religion that motivates them to become involved in anti-abortion or anti-nuclear activities?

The drug problem is a serious issue in this country because we talk and write about it. During the 1980's, President and Mrs. Reagan frequently appeared on TV to reiterate how serious the problem was. Words created a drug-conscious nation and even a solution to the problem. We convince ourselves that by talking and persuading each other, we are doing something about it. The words we use become our attitude toward the issue. We "say no to drugs." Note the word "say." We talk negatively about drugs and that becomes our action toward drugs. We say we are "fighting" the use of drugs. Words enable us to handle the issue and still sleep at night. This is not merely rhetoric, where the words don't fit the action, but language itself seen as action.

Denzin (1988) discusses the importance of language in creating self when he says, "In Heidegger, Sartre and Lacan, the self becomes a part of language, a pronoun only. Hence the center of the 'self' lies in language, not in interaction or social experience. It is language that shapes the direction experience takes."

Perinbanayagam (1985) argues that systems of signs become the material out of which "selves" are constituted. The relationship between selves is a relationship between one self and another in which the first is subject to himself and an object to the other and the second is subject to himself and an object to the first, simulataneously.

These examples show how linguistic analysis justifies certain behavior by creating a drama in which people participate. That is the crux of sociodrama. Sociodrama, like dramatism, seeks an analysis of the language used in discourse and its influence on human conduct.

---

## Axiom #3
*Social order is created as we talk about it —
in certain ways, for certain purposes, in certain roles,
in certain settings.*

---

As we have been defining the term here, sociodrama is a way of enlisting involvement and identification through the use of words. Duncan describes sociodrama in these words:

> Movies, radio, television, the popular press, all forms of modern mass communication, reach their greatest power in their creation of sociodramas, which, like art drama, are staged as struggles between good and bad principles of social order. The people do not want information about, but identification with, community life. In drama they participate.

We create meanings as we communicate. Communication is not a message track in which symbols become objects passing through that track. With such a view we "transact" meanings that are already established, but do not create them. Sociodrama is concerned with creating meanings as we become involved. If a relationship or group of people have no meaning for us, like a failing marriage or a company we no longer enjoy working for, it is because we do not identify ourselves as part of the social order. We talk as if that person or group no longer means anything to us, and, in that process, we become disconnected.

Duncan was concerned that students of human social behavior simply do not believe that how we communicate determines how we relate as social beings. Most people want to see some reality like power, authority, conflict, or consensus behind a symbol. It is how words are used that determine their social meaning. It is President Clinton's words that create consensus. People identify with him through the words and together Clinton and his followers create consensus. If people do not identify with him through his words, they see him tearing the country apart through his words.

Hall (1980) says that media messages have three kinds of responses from the audience member: acceptance, rejection, or negotiation. The audience does not simply accept, but depending on the culture of the audience member, he/she takes a particular stand. This is why Hall criticizes positivistic communication research in isolating elements in the audience like effects, uses, or gratifications. The messages are decoded according to the symbolic world of the audience member's culture.

The prevailing opinions of functionalist public relations experts view symbol-makers as ventriloquists' dummies. The speeches of political candidates — the *ways* in which they try to move people to vote — are considered for them a "reflection of interests" instead of ways of relating. In sociodrama, words that express who and what we are reflect the way we are held together. The Seabrook Nuclear Power Plant debates in New Hampshire polarized *people* - not Seabrook. The discourse of each side of the nuclear issue created communities of like-minded individuals — not the other way around. The actor in a drama creates meaning for others through language. Mead (1934) says the actor, however, is already part of a universe of discourse — he knows meaning or signification before the encounter.

Communication is an act in itself, made possible through the symbols of language. Perinbanayagam (1985) says, "The production of meaning must be viewed as an act, albeit an act that demands completion from self and/or others, whether it is a speech act or a written act."

---

**Axiom #4**

*Sociodrama is not concerned with how society persuades us, but how words about society persuade us to act in certain ways in our social relationships.*

---

We do not relate and then talk, we relate as we talk, and the forms of speech available to us determine how we relate as social beings. What we read and with whom we speak determines which way we relate to ourselves and those who are significant to us.

The communication theory implicit in the theory of sociodrama is an active, self-determining, and creative one. It is concerned with how symbols are used to create and sustain social order. Many people have said that society exists within communication. Sociodrama shows *how* that happens by emphasizing that symbols *constitute* social order. The kinds of symbols we have — the ways in which they are used, for what purposes, by what kinds of people, and in what kinds of acts — structure our relationships with each other. If how reality is expressed has little to do with how it functions in creating social order, communication becomes a residual, not a constitutive, category of social experience.

In sociodrama, public relations is not *like* a drama. It *is* a drama that calls forth the active involvement of the participants, and the involvement takes place through identification. As members of an audience, we identify with one another just as elements in a machine mesh or separate. Which is more dialogical? We want to identify with others. We want to be part of something. If we can identify ourselves with an organization, we become a part of it. They no longer communicate *to* us; we communicate with one another.

Identification is our response or action in the dramatic process called sociodrama. Duncan says,

> In times of transition, shifts in allegiance to symbols of authority are common. Problems of identity, not simply the need to belong but with whom to belong, become crucial. When men cannot act under one set of names they must choose others; how such choices are made is revealed in the symbolic phases of the struggle for new meanings. Identity is expressed as a glory, a mystical moment of belonging in which we commit ourselves to act under a certain name. These inner 'mysterious' moments must be expressed to become acts or attitudes, which are incipient acts. Thus, identification is always dependent on objectification through communication.

The concept of identification is rooted in the symbolic interactionist tradition, which advocates the discovery of self in and through communication. One does not have an identity and then communicate. Instead, one finds his identity through communication. Duncan paraphrases Mead when he says, "We act as we do because we communicate, not because

Figure 2: Sociodrama Matrix

*Levels  of  the  Drama*

| Elements of the Drama | a. Behind-the-Scenes | b. On Stage | c. Outside the Theater |
|---|---|---|---|
| 1. act | 1a | 1b | 1c |
| 2. scene | 2a | 2b | 2c |
| 3. means | 3a | 3b | 3c |
| 4. actors | 4a | 4b | 4c |
| 5. purpose | 5a | 5b | 5c |

we have drives or ideas first and then come together to express them. The self and society originate and develop in communication."

## Elements of the Drama

What is important in sociodrama is the concept of the presence of drama in our speech or writing The drama is our link with others. Language takes on a dramatic metaphor that forms our understanding, interpretation, and attitude toward the person, thing, or event about which we are speaking or writing.

---

**Axiom #5**

*We relate to each other through written or spoken words*
*which share the characteristics of drama.*

---

Perinbanyagam (1987) sets the stage for looking at symbols as drama when he says,

> All discourses can be critically examined in terms of texture and dramatic structures. ...Every cognition is derived from a previous cognition and in dramatic and narrative forms this derivation is the central defining principle.

Borrowing from Burke, Duncan introduces the pentad, or the five elements that make up the drama of discourse. These five major dramatic concepts, called "dramatic elements," are: ACT, SCENE, MEANS, ACTORS, and PURPOSE. As we talk or write, these elements are always present. (See Figure 2, previous page)

The **act** is what is done. It is society's celebration of social bonds; the transcendental occasions when society is reborn with an enactment of beliefs and values which its members, in general, accept. The Fourth of July is one example. Another example is the family get-together at holiday time. Love and hostility can both be experienced in the family get-together, but it rekindles affection and a sense of history for the family whose members are often isolated from one another during the rest of the year. The social order of family is reborn. We talk about the dinner long before we assemble and long after we have left one another. The act — the dinner — is not just a word, but a way of relating to one another.

The **scene** symbolizes time and place as a dramatic setting creating the proper conditions for social action. When we gather for a special dinner, the setting we want must be perfect: candles, china, wine, flowers. We discuss the way things should look for the occasion. We set the scene in language.

The **means** is the form of communication we use. The media can portray a certain message concerning the country, but can also, on occasion, link the country together. The return of the hostages from Iran in 1980 was a moment when television united the country and restored national hope, if only for a brief period of time. A shuttle success or disaster can do the same via media coverage. A handshake may provide a person with a sense of belonging. A memo, on the other hand, may provide a sense of isolation. A person interprets each form in terms of his relationship to a particular social order.

**Actors** refer to those who play certain roles for community purposes. The President of the United States presides over Memorial Day services at Arlington National Cemetery. Through him the country honors those who died during war. Our elders often preside at family get-togethers. Their power gives meaning to the event for ourselves and for others. As we arrange the seating at the table we do not simply recognize the power line, we create it.

Finally, **purpose** indicates the reasons we give for why we do what we do in this drama. It involves belief in certain values that may be considered necessary to community survival. The ERA struggle rallies around the premise that in our society women are equal to men. We talk about that purpose.

The press portrays the news in dramatic form, highlighting conflict, familiar heroes, and villains. To the media, O.J. Simpson was a villian, or fallen angel, long before any trial. Newsmen are involved in the creation of sociodrama, staging an eternal struggle between good and bad principles of social order. Edelman (1988) says a crisis, like all news developments, is a creation of the language used to depict it. The appearance of a crisis is a political act, not a recognition of fact or of a rare situation.

The drama is enacted, therefore, for the purposes of a particular social order. By acting in certain sociodramas, we uphold a particular order of human relationship. The enactment takes place through our choice of communication forms.

---

## Axiom #6
*Social interaction is not a process, but a dramatic expression, an enactment of roles by individuals who seek to identify with each other in their search to create social order.*

---

**Social order** is an important concept in sociodrama. Communication can build up, destroy, or threaten a particular kind of social order or structure of relationships. Television commercials in the United States, for example, are not just vehicles to sell products. They legitimize and promote the capitalist social order. Placed as they are in a setting of mass entertainment — enacted by certain personalities, at a particular time and in a particular program, sometimes with sophistication and creative genius — they persuade us to buy more than products. Badaracco (1990) shows us that one of the major consequences of commercial message delivery over the past century has been a change in the way Americans talk, write, read, behave, value, and believe. The message producers became the public relations profession.

## Hierarchy

---

### Axiom #7
*In public relations we create sociodramas which have a built-in hierarchy and with which the organization and the public both identify.*

---

Language expresses a certain hierarchy, which is another important concept within sociodrama. Perinbanayagam (1985) says, "Power, status, degrees of intimacy and changes in the character of ongoing relationships are all indicated by the grammatical forms chosen for the exchange of significant acts between relevant actors."

Social order involves people who communicate as superiors, inferiors, and equals, and pass from one position to another. We justify our rank to ourselves and to others at any particular time by enacting, in various kinds of community dramas, the value of some great transcendant principle of social order.

One company, for example, expects us to act in a certain way. A communication professional for the company is requested by the company to present this matter in a certain light. In complying we seek to uphold some great transcendent principle of social order.

The public relations person, who is a middle manager (hierarchy), has to report to a supervisor (hierarchy) and at the same time write a newsletter for the employees (hierarchy) so that they can serve clients (hierarchy) more effectively. Each person or group of persons represents a certain positioning in the organization. We are not the same audience and our needs are not the same in regard to the organization.

What is important to remember is that the organization could not function without that hierarchy. A simple newsletter becomes a way to create, justify, and sustain a hierarchy through which the organization functions. At a recent conference on direct marketing, McCarthy (1994) said to use the newsletter as a vehicle of dialogue with one's customers.

Give the reader a chance to respond. 'Relationship marketing' is a new name for direct marketing. Each level recognizes the others, and that is done not telepathically, but through the newsletter as discourse. Sociodrama helps us see that the organization and its structure are born and sustained through an intricate system of communication forms with which the various constituents of the organization identify.

A Honeywell Company study showed how various employees read the company newsletter according to their own needs: supervisors, to make sure their message is coming across; achievers, to find out if there are any new openings in the company; and socialites, to find out what's happening in the lives of other employees, like new births and marriages. Each audience reads the same newsletter differently because each level is creating and justifying its position in the organization through decoding the newsletter according to individual needs. Duncan says, "In a democratic society, struggle for public approval becomes a competitive drama in which the audience [the public] is considered part of the action, not simply a passive mass."

Social order is always a resolution of the struggle between superiors, inferiors, and equals. This struggle takes the form of a great community drama in which, through comedic as well as tragic means, the community seeks to ward off threats to the majesty of its transcendent symbols of social integration. *Skill in playing hierarchical roles is determined by skill in hierarchical address.* The actor in the social drama of hierarchy must please his superiors, inspire his inferiors, and convince his equals. The emphasis on both verbal and writing skills in public relations training, therefore, is well advised. The public relations professional tries to articulate the company's interests both for the company and for its audiences. This point provides a strong argument for keeping public relations education in the communications department, where skills can become a focus of the educational process. Goldman (1988) points out that drug ads in medical magazines positioned the doctor in terms of the patient and his manic depression. There was a drama enacted through the ad that became the social order called medical intervention. One may have trouble with the way the social order is structured, but that also needs to be symbolized in some way: e.g. consumer protest, union movement, or investigative journalism.

Sociodrama proposes that we use **forms** to create a certain kind of social order, but that the forms are expressed in a hierarchical context. We appeal to a higher power and are part of that social order at the same time. For example, a long-standing furniture store in Boston promotes itself through the history of its early struggle to provide good service and its present need to live up to that great history.

Public relations takes expression in the discourse of writing and speaking that, in turn, enables audiences to play a role in the organization. In a dramatistic study of fire fighters, Cragen and Shields (1981) show that public relations and a good public image are synonymous with a "higher power" for fire fighters. *The style of writing* shows a hierarchy that justifies and validates a certain social order, which in this case is the fire department. More than a justification, the words can also create the kind of fire department it is. In this study, public relations activities are the means to an end, the road to salvation, and the way to expiate past sins, all rolled into one. *The writing* enables the organization to take a certain form, e.g., we are a fire department that seeks to serve the public good, and in that service we find our reason for being.

We do not simply *do* public relations. When we link sociodrama to public relations, we are talking about actors, both inside and outside the organization, creating a social order in a certain way through language.

## Three Levels of Sociodrama as Communication

In public relations, messages are produced and distributed through some form of media, whether interpersonal, group, or technology-based. Discourse between participants can occur on three different levels. Each level corresponds to where we see the drama being played, either **behind-the-scenes** (concerning the producers), **on-stage** (concerning the audience), or **outside the theater** (concerning the outside actors with whom the audience interacts). (See Figure 2)

The first level is behind-the-scenes, which involves the actors in an organization making a decision regarding the message to be used. The actors could be the public relations director and the writer, who choose not only the content but the form. The timing and setting for distribution is also up to them. For example, their reasons for choosing one piece of news over another is frequently based on management policy, but can also be based on their need to say something, even to themselves. Finally, they must decide to whom it should go.

What is important to notice in behind-the-scenes sociodrama is that the actors (public relations director, producers, writers, artists, photographers) attach meaning to their work. That meaning may be based on a desire to be number one in the market or just a need to get the job done today. There could, in other words, be any number of reasons why they choose to say one thing rather than another, but their motives are wrapped up in their communication. **Actors justify their way of acting in communication.**

We, the "audience" who receives the message, have images or ideas about what may have happened behind-the-scenes. We can imagine how the story in the newsletter originated, under what setting it was written, why it was written, why certain words were used, and why the writer talks about one person rather than another. All of these are the elements of the sociodrama called "newsletter." So it is with most of the gossip in any organization, which is merely a communication form that enables actors to feel part of the organization (Heilman).

The second level is **on-stage**, which involves an audience paying attention to our message. The recipients of the message, either viewers or readers, see or hear that message and attach meaning to it. Sometimes that meaning can be quite different from what the public relations staff had in mind. The message is received at a certain time and place which may be different from person to person. For example, the news serves different purposes for each person, ranging from entertainment to information or a combination of each. The audience uses the language of the writer to identify with the drama that is being created.

---

### Axiom #8
*The recipients of the messages we create and send are active viewers, listeners, or readers.*

---

The recipients of our message need to make sense of their lives, and our communication media provide them with a vehicle. They acknowledge and absorb messages according to their needs. When they read the newsletter, they use the information as they need to, but not necessarily the same way the writer intended. Their discussions of the newsletter are one expression of their use of that newsletter. Thayer (1979) argues that the talk about communication media *is* the effect of media on our lives. Talk is necessary to become and remain an organization. Discussions happen because they express involvement and identification. A good question to research within sociodrama would certainly be "What kind of sociodramatic talk is going on within our organization— gossip, a newsletter, media coverage, a brochure, a meeting, or a speech?" Talking is the primary way in which our audiences create their image of the organization and the way they relate to it.

The third level of sociodrama is **outside-the-theater**. Here we view the relationships of the recipients of the message to the larger social order. The actors interpret the message for their own needs and then interpret it for others such as family, friends, the neighborhood, the city, the country, etc. They relate the message to themselves *and* to others, thus creating a sociodrama. By talking about it, they give it value for themselves. They order their world in and through the message. By identifying with the message, they create their own drama of the organization in relation to their wider social environment.

Writers and public relations professionals interact to produce a message, readers and viewers interact with the communication form, and viewers interact with their world of friends and associates. Sociodrama shows that communication forms human relationships on each level. Television and the press do not *do something* to us in the way a needle injects an arm. Instead, they create sociodramas. Like all good drama, they portray struggles between good and bad principles of social order and we participate in that struggle. Perinbanayagam (1985) says, "Meaning is produced between reflective actors through discursive acts, and significances are waves that move between and among them."

---

### Axiom #9
*We identify with victims, scapegoats, and stereotypes in interpreting the messages in public relations strategies and thus create images concerning the organization as it relates to us.*

---

To sum up, public relations is not about getting the message out there. Public relations is understanding human interaction under certain conditions and providing a message which is significant to the participants, in a particular form, for the purpose of social order. Sociodramas legitimize a certain social order.

---

### Axiom #10
*Communication, and public relations specifically, does not involve giving someone a message, but instead identifies with others in a common drama.*

---

We need public relations to identify with an organization. Sociodrama explains the way we identify with it. We imagine, we talk, we write in dramatic forms, and these forms of communication become the way we relate to each other, not simply the way we get a message to others. Again, Perinbanayagan (1987) says:

> In the discourses of everyday life, be they in the form of conversation, stories, or games, a self is created, its intentionalities experienced, announced, and asserted and an effect created in the world. This is achieved most parsimoniously and successfully, and often with a style and an elan, by using the resources of narrative and drama and proving solace to the lonely and the bored.

Life is neither theater nor is it different from theater. It is "theater-like." Sociodrama is a description of the language behavior of human beings who use theatrical (expressive) means to build their worlds. In many respects, they regard the world as so serious that the last thing they would call it is "theater." This is but one of the many paradoxes and riddles of sociodramatic thinking. Notwithstanding such criticism, sociodrama is a way for us to understand language and its relationship to social order.

# References

Adler, M.J. (1983). *How to speak, how to listen*. New York: Macmillan.

Badaracco, C. (1990 Publicity and Modern Influence. *Public Relations Review*, Vol 16, 3, Fall, pp. 5-18.

Blyler, N.R. (1992). Shared meaning and Public Relations Writing. *Journal of Technical Writing and Communication*. Vol 22, 3, p. 301-318.

Boden, D. (1990) People are Talking: Conversation Analysis and Symbolic Interaction. *Symbolic Interaction and Cultural Studies*. Edited by Howard S. Becker and Michael M. McCall. Chicago: University of Chicago Press.

Brissett, D. and Edgley, C., Eds. (1990). *Life as Theatre: A Dramaturgical Sourcebook*. 2nd Ed. New York: Aldine De Cruyter.

Burke, K. (1966) *Language as Symbolic Action: Essays on Life, Literature, and Method*. Berkeley: University of California Press.

Burke, K. (1968). Dramatism. In D.L. Sills (Ed.), *International encyclopedia of the social sciences*, pp. 445-451. New York: Macmillan.

Burrell, G., & Morgan, G. (1979). *Sociological paradigms and organizational analysis. Elements of the sociology of corporate life*. Portsmouth, NH: Heinemann.

Carragee, K. M. (1990). Interpretive media study and interpretive social science. *Critical Studies in Mass Communication*. Vol. 7, p. 81-96.

Cragan, J.F., & Shields, D.C. (1981). *Applied communication research: A dramatistic approach.* Prospect Heights, Il: Waveland Press.

Davis, F. (1981) On the 'symbolic' in interaction. *Symbolic Interaction*, 5 (1), pp. 111-126.

Denzin N. (1988). Art, Language, and Self in symbolic interactionist thought. *Studies in Symbolic Interaction.* Edited by Norman K. Denzin, Vol 9, pp. 51-80.

Duncan, H.D. (1985). *Communication and social order.* New Brunswick, U.S.A.: Transaction Books.

Duncan, H.D. (1967). *The search for a theory of communication in American sociology.* In F.E. Dance (Ed.), Human communication theory: Original essays (pp, 236-263). New York: Holt, Rinehart and Winston.

Edelman, M. (1988). *Constructing the Political Spectacle.* Chicago: University of Chicago Press

Gitlin, T. (1980). *The whole world is watching: Mass media in the making & unmaking of the New Left.* Berkeley: University of California Press.

Goffman, E. (1974). *Frame analysis: An essay on the organization of experience.* Cambridge, MA: Harvard University Press.

Goodman, N. (1978). *Ways of Worldmaking.* Indianapolis: Hacket Publishing, Co.

Gusfield, J. (1976). The literary rhetoric of science: Comedy and pathos in drinking and driving research. *American Sociological Review*, 41, 16-34.

Hall, S., Ed. (1980). Encoding/decoding. *Culture, Media, Language.* Working papers in cultural studies, 1972-79. London: University of Birminghan, pp. 128-138.

Heath, R. L. (1993) A rhetorical approach to zones of meaning and organizational prerogatives. *Public Relations Review.* Vol. 19, 2, Summer, p. 141-155.

Heilman, S.C. (1976). Synagogue life; *A study in symbolic interaction.* Chicago: University of Chicago Press.

Hellweg, S.A. (1989). *The Application of Grunig's Symmetry-Asymmetry Public Relations Models to Internal Communication Systems.* Paper presented to the International Communication Association, San Fransisco.

Kuhn, M.H. (1964). Major trends in symbolic interaction in the past twenty-five years. *Sociological Quarterly*, 5 (1), 61-84.

MacCannell, D. and MacCannell, J.F. (1982) *The time of the sign: Semiotic interpretation of modern culture.* Bloomington: Indiana University Press.

Mangham, I.L., and Overington, M.A. (1990). Dramatism and the Theatrical Metaphor. *Life as Theater.* 2nd Edition. Edited by Dennis Brissett and Charles Edgley. New York: Aldine De Gruyter.

Mead, G.H. (1934). *Mind, self and society: From the standpoint of a social behaviorist.* Chicago: University of Chicago Press.

McCarthy, B. (1994). Lecture: *Marketing Communication in the Information Economy.* May 12, Westin Hotel, sponsored by PRSA Yankee Chapter, Waltham, MA.

Mickey, T.J. (1980). Social order and preaching. *Social Compass*, XXVII (4), 347-362.

Overington, M.A. (1977). Kenneth Burke as social theorist. *Sociological Inquiry*, 47 (2), 138.

Perinbanaygam, R.S. (1985). *Signifying Acts: Structure and meaning in everyday life*. Carbondale: Southern Illinois University Press.

Perinbanayagam, R.S. (1987). Drama in Everyday Life. *Studies in Symbolic Interaction*, Vol 8, p 125-140.

Rogers, E.M. (1994). *A History of Communication Study: A Biographical Approach*. New York: Free Press.

Rosengren, K.E. (1983). Communication research: One paradigm, or four? *Journal of Communication*, 33 (3), 188.

Rosengren, K.E. (1993). From Field to Frog Ponds. *Journal of Communication*. Summer 1993, Vol. 43, No. 3, p. 6-17.

Rueckert, W.H. (1963). *Kenneth Burke and the drama of human relations*. Minneapolis: University of Minnesota Press.

Thayer, L. (1979). On the mass media and mass communication: Notes toward a theory. In R.W. Budd and B.D. Ruben (Eds.), *Beyond media: New approaches to mass communication*. Rochelle Park, NJ: Hayden.

Young, T.R. (1990). *The Drama of Social Life: Essays in Post-Modern Social Psychology*. New Brunswick: Transaction Books.

# Chapter 3

# Public Relations as Sociodrama

## The Language of Public Relations

So far, we have looked at sociodrama and have seen the theory expressed via the ten axioms. Now we want to establish a clearer connection with public relations.

Though she equates public relations with publicity, Badarracoo (1990) points out the importance of language and language products, such as the brochure or news story, in giving public relations its modern importance. Badaracco says that the stage of public relations from 1945 to the present is called the "control phase," where public relations professionals joined management in order to exert control over the corporate environment and instill values consistent with public images and cultural narratives. They harnessed the flow of information that reached the public, maintaining balance between the interests of the corporation and public access to economic truth-telling. The resultant product was cultural liaison, social harmony, an interested audience, and corporate well-being. Tradesmen were now executives—those who expedited orders—and were removed from production details. The public relations professional changed from a tradesman to an executive who served the public interest or at least tried to better position the product or service of the company in light of that interest. Badaracco's argument centers on the importance of public relations language and its impact on culture.

A public relations staff and its audiences create sociodramas in their discourse about an organization. They use the elements and interact among the levels of sociodrama in writing and talking about the organization. Both parties experience involvement in a drama as they interact with each other.

An interpretive approach to communication centers on communication forms, particularly the use of language in writing and speaking. As Stuart Hall (1975) says,

> Against the main weight of sociological practice, we approached the news-
> paper [in this book, public relations material whether spoken or written]
> as a structure of meanings, rather than as a channel for the transmission
> and reception of news [or information].

In sociodrama, the focus is not just with style, but with symbol and
the meanings it generates as a way of connecting with each other within a
particular social order. Style seems to imply an ephemeral 'how' we do
things. Using the sociodrama model, we use words (how we express ourselves) not simply to get a message across but to relate to one another
within a given context. It is a question of *content as form* in sociodrama.
We are symbol-using creatures and, as Duncan has pointed out, the symbols we use define who we are and what our aspirations are for one another. The forms we use in communication are ways that we motivate
first ourselves and then others. Denzin (1988) writes that language is the
fundamental causal factor in the genesis of self.

The key terms in sociodrama theory are:

| | |
|---|---|
| symbol | persuasion |
| social order | drama |
| communication | hierarchy |
| language | image |

Each of these terms is important in understanding the theory of
sociodrama, and therefore important when looking at public relations from
that perspective.

When the public relations activity of an organization is performed
(i.e. when anyone speaks or writes about a company), it is done within
the context of both the **elements** and the **levels** of a drama. According to
Perinbanyagam (1985), the analysis of social life is inadequate if it is not
treated, to begin with, as drama and only then compared to other forms
and paradigms. We create images of the organization along the same dramatic lines. Through its language we interpret the organization as it relates to us and then interpret it for others.

A former President of the Public Relations Society of America explains:

> Public relations is aimed at maintaining the legitimacy of a company or
> industry, a perception by the public that the company or industry is oper-
> ating in the public interest and is serving a social need. (1981)

He implies that public relations includes making the company acceptable to the public. This can only be accomplished when people talk about the organization in their own words. Society can not accept something unless it's members can talk about it. Language becomes the way to express acceptance and be part of the organization or its mission. Language is the symbol or form through which actors interact. It is that form about which sociodrama is concerned. Language which may not always be *official* communication provides us with involvement in the organization.

Symbol or form creates a particular kind of social order through interaction between the actors in a drama. Actors choose to relate to each other through symbol and that symbol helps define who they are. This process or exchange is sociodrama: form or symbol within the context of a drama.

For public relations, the elements of the drama appear in how we write and talk about the organization. We don't just *talk*. We use dramatic discourse that involves others and ourselves in the organization.

The five elements of dramatic discourse discussed in Chapter 2 are present in public relations language: the act, the scene, the means, the actors, and the purpose.

The **act** involves the deed — as we perceive and talk about it — that our organization has executed. The American Cancer Society works to improve the health of the nation when it conducts its annual Great American Smokeout. The Phillip Morris corporation argues for the rights of Americans in its "Right To Smoke" discourse. The company sponsored a national road show display of an actual copy of the Bill of Rights to support that argument. Chrysler claims that it acts to support the American auto worker when the company lobbies for fewer foreign car imports.

The **actors** are the individuals we see portrayed in this process. Tylenol became a victim when someone tampered with their pain reliever boxes. In subsequent Tylenol promotions, both print and broadcast, the individuals who spoke for the product were men and women with whom we could identify. They experienced renewed confidence in Tylenol and so could we. They were not simply promoting a product, but creating a drama in which a victim is first portrayed and then rescued by a believable hero. We became actors in that drama as we responded to the message. We became the hero for Tylenol's rescue.

The **agency** is the means the organization uses to speak to its audiences. If a boss sends an employee a memo, instead of speaking to him personally, the employee gets a message that goes beyond the memo.

McLuhan's phrase, "The medium is the message," might be appropriate here. Different dramas are played out when we interact with a memo and when we interact with a person.

The media form structures the way we understand ourselves, the organization, and our relationship with it. The agency is not neutral. For example, in the age of AIDS and other sexually transmitted diseases, people use computer technology for their sexual needs and call it Cybersex (Molnar, 1994). Sexologists, working in conjunction with scientists and other serious people, are creating a complex, woven fabric of trillions of super-sensitive fibers that can mimic the action and sensations of human flesh. Today technology mediates our sexual needs and so we think we need not fear STD's. In that choice of means, might we not be alienating ourselves from the joys of human contact? The means we use define ourselves.

The **scene** involves discussion of the environment or setting in which the social order is created or established. In selling a new car, we advertise the car in a desert setting with the stereotype of a beautiful woman in hopes that the consumer will fantasize being alone with the woman and then buy the car. The union of solitary buyer and the setting create a sense that this is an important way to link with the car manufacturer. How bland (actually impossible, without some kind of sociodrama) it would be to simply "sell" a car. In this example, the manufacturer works to create a sense of independence, privacy, and uniqueness by getting the buyer to identify with the scene through language and picture.

The element of **purpose** is the statement of values or motivation implicit in the social order that is being created through a promotional campaign. The continuance of beautiful, green forests was the purpose behind the "Smokey the Bear" campaign. We need one another for this lofty goal. Many people seek the goal of maintaining places that are unpolluted and accessible like our state forests. We have a common purpose. When we see the Smokey TV spots or read the press promotion, we become part of a drama which has a common purpose. Smokey is working for and with us as WE try to stamp out forest fires. Animal rights groups work to create a world in which every living being, animal and human, has rights. Cosmetics that are not tested on animals have become a big market because the value of animal rights is being respected.

In the sociodrama view of public relations, we can also talk about the different levels within a drama. Through our writing and speaking we refer to the drama as it happens on the three different levels of action: behind-the-scenes, on-stage, and outside-the-theater.

A particular social order is created by the actors **behind-the-scenes**, which is the first level on which the drama takes place. As the former PRSA president indicated, the first question of legitimacy is of the company or industry to itself. The company wants to see itself as important. Managers and public relations professionals in the organization talk, and in their interaction they make decisions as to what to say or not say to their external audiences.

The consumer, or external audience, talks about what goes on behind the scenes, just as the people directly involved in the company talk about what happens on that same level. We have images of who is making decisions and why they are making them. The images may be right or wrong, but it is the *talk about the company itself that is important* [Axiom #1]. Some anti-smoking activists would argue that all the tobacco company executives want to increase their annual revenue at the expense of public health. They portray those leading the company in a certain way and consider them to be "behind-the-scenes" players.

Another social order is created with external audiences with whom we interact as representatives of a company or industry, and this second level of the drama is called **on-stage**. The public relations practitioner is concerned with the perception of the company by the external audience. A social order is created by that audience as it interprets the company or industry.

In the never-ending battle against foreign auto imports, Chrysler insists that America can employ more people and that companies do not have to import from overseas to succeed. People interpret the meaning of Chrysler for themselves based on their needs.

For many, Chrysler *is* America. Lee Iacocca is revered as a promoter of the American dream. His involvement in the restoration of the Statue of Liberty and an earlier national discussion about his possible candidacy for the Presidency are other ways to link the consumer to the American dream. In reading and talking about a company, the public can identify with certain qualities in the company itself or in a representative of the company. They either find meaning in it for themselves or not.

The third level of drama within public relations is called **outside-the-theater** and concerns the social order created by various external audiences. In our discourse, we project that people out there understand us and what we do. They project, for example, what the nuclear plant will mean for the local community, just as the people inside the plant project a value or benefit with having the plant there. Our discussion of *out there* is a way of relating and creating a link between the organization and the public.

Sociodrama is concerned with the public's image or perception of the organization in their dealings with other people in the community. Members of that public enact a drama in their talk about the company with others and thus the company becomes hero, villain, mystery, victim, or savior. People interact with others about the company precisely because the company becomes a topic of discussion or a way of relating and, as a result, becomes important to them. The more they talk about the company, the more important it becomes to them. That is why it is important to know what people are saying. It is in that discourse that the company is accepted or rejected. Discussion about the organization creates all kinds of images that are projected on the outside: acceptance, questions, service, value, importance, or waste.

Public relations, therefore, is not just publicity (or agency) but a drama that is enacted in speech on three different levels within and outside a company or organization.

We do not just spread information. We communicate ourselves. We find identificatio.We create a certain kind of social order through our words and sociodrama enables us to find meaning within that order.

A real discovery of "self" goes on within sociodrama. The company discovers its "self" through exchanges among its members. The company, in reaching its external audiences, gives those audiences an opportunity to relate (i.e. discover the meaning for themselves) to the company. The audiences, in turn, portray themselves to others along with the meanings that they have taken from the interaction with the company. In knowing what people are talking about, a company knows how much people accept it.

Sociodrama as an interpretive approach is a humanistic view of communication because it looks at language as a way to create relationships rather than as a way to get a message across. It helps us move away from the strongly manipulative assumption so frequently present in definitions of public relations. Sociodrama is interactive and emphasizes a humanistic basis for public relations.

Since there is no one theory of public relations and what does exist in basic texts in public relations is frequently positivist, it is important to present a theory that is both humanistic and more dialogical.

Sociodrama lends itself to understanding public relations because of its emphasis on the spontaneity, intuition, and creativity present when we communicate with one another. We do not always know how people both inside and outside the organization talk about us. That talk is the way they relate to their friends, their superiors, their enemies, the media, and themselves.

Communication is not a given, but a creation of actors, interacting by defining themselves in and through discourse. Sociodrama helps one see that we come together in that interaction by the ways we choose to relate. The ways are frequently the words we use in writing and speaking. Words, or language, make possible a certain kind of social order [Axiom #3].

Words about the organization are always expressed in terms of imagery. We have images that we create through our conversations with others. Therefore, the sociodrama enacted between individuals takes the form of certain kinds of imagery which is expressed in the language they use. For example, we might speak of Tylenol as a company that has had a good track record, but also had an unfortunate accident. We might picture Tylenol "as American as apple pie" since its parent company is Johnson and Johnson, and therefore expect it will be around a long time. In both of these sentences about Tylenol we have images of victim and hero. We don't just talk. We talk in imagery. When we say "Tylenol," we have an image in our minds and filter what we say about it through that image. The concept of imagery is important for public relations.

It is clear that sociodrama is a theory with which to better understand public relations activity. We use dramatic metaphors in our discourse about a company or organization. Those metaphors involve us. They are not just tools to express how we think and feel, but are ways of involving both management and any internal or external audience. Sociodrama is not concerned with how "society" persuades us, but how words about society persuade us to act in certain ways in our social relationships [Axiom #4].

Using the sociodrama model, professionals do not look for the right word to say or write, but a word that will *involve* the reader or the listener. A word that creates involvement is one that evokes an image for the listener or reader. Public relations professionals need to be attuned to the kinds of images people have of the organization and, specifically, how that imagery comes across in the language they use when speaking about the organization.

## Image and Sociodrama

Assume for a moment, through the interpretive view of sociodrama, that the people or audience we are trying to reach create their own meanings [Axiom #8]. An obvious implication for the public relations profession is that the people or public have certain images of public relations and public relations work. We need to know what those images are so that we can talk to members of those audiences and understand them while working toward being understood ourselves.

There is a significant link between sociodrama and "image"—an important word in marketing, advertising, and public relations practice as well.

The way we perceive something is related to what we have learned about it in other settings. In other words, understanding *how* we came to know what we know is an important part of understanding perception. We are able to "perceive" because we know what to look for from earlier learning experiences. When we do not know, or fail to perceive something, it is because we have not experienced it in the past. One might describe the perception itself as an "image." We have images of people and things that enable us to perceive them. Images are born, sustained, and changed through discourse. Herbert Blumer (1979), a symbolic interactionist pioneer, said, "The meaning of objects for a person arises fundamentally out of the way they are defined to him by others with whom he interacts."

An image originates and hinges on the ability of the actors to talk about and thus construct an image. We do not just get images from thin air—we get them through our conversations with others, by our own reading, and by listening to others.

Once we have images, we tend to use them to guide or "frame" the way we relate to people and things. Lippman (1945) equates subjective reality with images, or what he calls "pictures in people's heads". Boulding (1966) calls the image subjective knowledge that governs behavior. He says,

> Persons themselves are to a considerable extent what their images make them. Because the image is a creation of the message, people tend to remake themselves in the image which other people have of them. Personal relations, therefore, involve an extremely complex action and reaction of images upon images. If I think that Mr. A is a mean individual, I will treat him in such a way that he will become meaner.

Adoni and Mane (1983) define the social construction of reality as a process that includes interactions among individuals, society, and culture. They argue we externalize our own internalized and subjective meanings, experiences, and actions. Their work seems to parallel the discussion of an interpretive theory of public relations in which the subjects create their own images and meanings toward the organization through discourse.

Dan Nimmo (1974), in his work in political communication, gives more detail on how images are created. He talks about how verbal and non-verbal symbols that politicians and their audiences use create the image of the political candidate. He brings definition to Boulding's work by pointing out that it is through a symbolic process between the actors that we arrive at our images. One can describe that process as a drama of communication. The dramatistic form is the groundwork for understanding how we come to have the images we have. We don't just create images; we create them as little dramas that take on bigger meanings for us.

The drama can be called sociodrama because it is intended to create, preserve, or destroy a certain kind of social order. For example, one might say "This is what I think the company is," and then act toward the company in keeping with that image. Even if the action is contrary to the language used, the fact that the organization was spoken about in a certain way defines the relationship with the organization at that time. Even statements of objectivity are filled with feelings about the organization.

The drama of spoken and written communication is the source of the images we have. If we can understand the elements of the drama, we will be better equipped to understand how the drama works. Images are created when we're interacting with our friends, co-workers, the media, or the boss, in both the elements and levels of sociodrama.

As we have seen, sociodrama is enacted in images on three different levels. First, one might image the drama taking place behind the scenes. An individual can have an idea of what management does and for what purposes in the hidden chambers of the boardroom. Second, one might imagine the drama on stage. This is the image that directly effects the audience at a particular time. Images of a civil greeting from a superior create an expectation around that event. Images are built up in sociodrama regarding place and time for this greeting. Third, one might image the drama as outside the theater. This refers to the images we have of what others out there are going to think of us or of the company. Our imagination may enact how bad we will look in the community if we do not allow the United Way campaigners to come into the office to solicit this year.

Images are dramas we enact in the imagination for the purpose of sustaining or creating a social order with which we identify. As Nimmo (1974) points out, political public relations professionals use imagery in their work to promote a candidate:

> The political rhetoric and imagery of candidates typically celebrates the origin and destiny of the political order. The imagery of campaign ads—

portrayed in both pictorial and verbal communication—reminds voters of deeply held symbols.

Though Nimmo argues that people can be sold anything and even contradictory things through political publicity, he makes a strong case for our dependence on images and the myths to which they belong. Another definition for myth might be a drama that we enter into as one of the actors. We do not just want *any* politician. We want someone who will represent *us*, who will stand for what *we* think is important, and who will take *our* message to Congress. Notice there is always a self-reference point in our relationship with the politician. We find ourselves involved in that discourse. That is the approach of both dramatism and symbolic interactionism which provide the basis for sociodrama.

It is often through storytelling that we hear the images of the company or organization. The stories are told by the company, within the company, by the customers of the company, and by any other audience who relates to the company for some reason. The stories are full of imagery that people use to describe their experience with the organization. The images are important sources of motivation for people. If the stories are tampered with, we have tampered with their security and perhaps their lifeline.

Any time the company must communicate, it is done in story. Any time we communicate with each other, we communicate in story. We say, "Let me tell you what happened to me today." The stories are filled with the five elements and three levels of drama mentioned earlier. A real *collection* or *mosaic* of images of the organization exists that people develop based on their own individual needs and use to relate to the organization.

## Image as Mosaic

By mosaic we mean the *super-image* that the various internal and external audiences together create concerning the organization. They do not see the same organization, but rather a piece of the organization which is an image they have developed of the organization. That image is expressed in dramatic metaphors.

The relationship between discourse about the organization and the image of the organization needs to be explored further. Does talk precede image, accompany image, or follow image?

People want to be associated with one another, therefore there must be a common image. On some level, we must share the image of an organization with certain audiences. Reference group theory says that we identify with groups of people in just about everything we do. Shibutani (1975) puts it this way:

> The concept of 'reference group' has been used in several ways, but its utility can be maximized when it signifies that group whose presumed perspective is used by an actor as the frame of reference in the organization of his perceptual field.

The same would hold for the image of an organization. Though various groups identify with an organization, we tend to cling to the organization with people who think like us. We share the same images. There is not just one audience. There is a collection of audiences with which any single organization must interact.

Communication is interaction between actors who share a similar image. That communication tends to enhance a particular image and thus a specific way of acting or behavior toward the organization.

In a study of the automobile industry by the Chrysler Corporation (Katen, 1984), customers were asked to rank a particular car according to its youthfulness, luxury, or practicality. The customers expressed their image of the car by the way they positioned that car in relation to other Chrysler cars. The four poles of the two axes were: has a touch of class and very practical; and, conservative looking and sporty looking. Envision the images on a map (what we call here a **mosaic**). The map consists of two axes, and the four poles are labeled: "touch of class," "very practical," "conservative-looking," and "sporty-looking." In the Chrysler study, each car was imaged in a different spot. The customers were looking at Chrysler by seeing a particular car with which they identified, but they were not all looking at the same Chrysler organization. They were interested in Chrysler only as it pertained to them and their needs or interests.

We can understand an organization's image by talking with representatives from each audience within the organization. That was the purpose of a study done by William Stephenson (1963), on the image of a public utility company. The task was to measure the images housewives have about utilities. What a woman feels about utilities is made up of past conversations, perceived objects, experiences with utility companies and department stores, advertisements, and their thoughts about the issue when asked. In-depth interviews were conducted. Housewives were encouraged to talk freely about themselves in relation to utilities, their uses, and appliances as associated with the city's stores, public institutions, the mass media, and any other influence.

Two images emerged from the research. The first showed a friendliness to utilities in a corporate sense, with little that was personal to themselves as housewives. They looked at utilities in terms of economics. The second image suggested an image of service to the housewife, and indifference to utilities in a corporate sense. Those housewives depend on services provided or expected. Stephenson says, the images "reflect the women's way of looking at things, and it is safe to infer that the women will tend to act the way they look."

A similar study was recently conducted on the images of country western music in a large mid-western community (Smith, 1994). Stephenson's metholology in the utilities case was used.

The manifestation of an organization's influence is what people talk about. The ability of people to talk about an organization is a reflection of how people see the organization and act toward it. The conversation both stems from and influences the images that people have of the organization.

Can we be certain that image influences behavior? In discourse concerning the organization, one sees patterns or clusters of attitudes, opinions, or ideas. It is these attitudes, opinions, and ideas that influence the behavior of the participants. It is important to understand those patterns or clusters of images in order to deal effectively in public relations. Stephenson (1963) likens the situation to a medical doctor conducting an operation. We need to know

> the evaluation of a body of opinion as to its morphology, that is, the segments composing it. It would be invaluable for those considering a program [in public relations] to have such evaluations. Indeed, otherwise, they are in the position of physicians, about to operate on a body, who are ignorant of its parts.

Take another example. An employee says he feels his company takes care of him. His words (flowing from the image and, at the same time, creating the image) are framed in terms of the care and support he feels he has received. His opinion of the company is reflected strongly in his discussion of it. His image of the organization is portrayed by the words he uses, the things he repeats, the emphasis he gives, how his words interact with the words of other people who may have other attitudes than his, how he defends himself and his opinions, and how he projects himself as he talks about the organization. There may be a big difference between one person's image of an organization and what the organization actually is, but the customer's image cannot be ignored. The important concept is that *we act toward the organization the way we imagine it, because that's the way it 'is' for us.*

The image is a part of the mosaic that becomes the source for our understanding of and discourse about an organization. We only see one part of the mosaic, however, which is our part. In fact, each audience sees a different part of the mosaic. All the audiences that we can identify can have a different way of imagining the organization. Together they create the super-image or **organizational mosaic**. Because we need to link with others, the images are not infinite but can be viewed as several held by different groups or audiences. The image we hold is important largely because we say "I'm not the only one who thinks this way."

One form of behavior exhibited toward an organization is verbal behavior. We use language to be expressive and add form to the images we have of an organization. One does not have to be initially concerned with how one *acts* toward the organization if you can recognize *words* as an activity or form of behavior.

How do we avoid the problem of separating words from action? Sociodrama theory views words *as* action. Participants do not talk and then act. They act with their words. This sheds new light on an assumption which states "one's actions are louder than words." Discourse about a company or organization is an action concerning both the participants and the organization. Discourse indicates attitudes and feelings. Discourse also helps form those attitudes and opinions. Language is not an instrument to send out an idea. It is a way of forming oneself and one's world [Axiom #10].

If a company *says* it is responsible to the community and it really isn't, how can we believe the company? The company has positioned itself as unrelated to what it says it will do. The language has been used as a smoke screen and mystifies the public.

On the other hand, unless an organization *talks* about its work, the public has no idea that anything is being done. Again, discourse affirms both the organization and its internal audience, and informs its external audiences. The talk forms their images of the organization. The language is used as a formative element in the relationships among members of different audiences.

Ideas are not the *product* of discussion. Ideas are developed *as* we talk, just as organizations are developed through discussion, in both written or spoken form.

If discourse is viewed as a method of acting, the dichotomy so frequently introduced between action and word can be avoided. An organization that says it is willing to comply with EPA requirements and continues to dump dangerous chemicals into local water sources certainly speaks in both word and action. Their communication is, of course, contradictory and will ultimately alienate a large segment of the public. People relate to an organization as they talk about it, often in relation to what their friends and the media have to say. As a company continues to say one thing and do another, its audiences discuss the situation and become doubtful of the company's credibility. **An organization rises and falls on the strength of its public image which is the discourse among its various audiences.**

If your words, as a public relations professional, are to induce people to buy a product or service, those words have to interact with the image that the public holds of that product or service. The private discussions of customers/consumers must become part of the public discussion within the public relations campaign.

# References

Adoni, H. and Mane, S. (1983). Media and the social construction of reality: Toward an integration of theory and research.*Communication Research.* 11:323-340.

Badarraco, C. (1990). Publicity and Modern Influence. *Public Relations Review.* Vol. 16, 3, Fall, pp. 5-18.

Blumer, H. (1979). The symbolic significance of behavior. In C.D.

Mortensen (Ed.), *Basic readings in communication theory* (2nd ed.). New York: Harper & Row.

Boulding, K.E. (1956). *The image: Knowledge in life and society.* Ann Arbor: University of Michigan Press.

Denzin, N. (1988). Art, Language, and the Self. *Studies in Symbolic Interaction.* Vol. 9.

Hall, S. (1975). Introduction to A.C. Smith et al., *Paper voices.* Washington, D.C.: Rowant & Littlefield Publications, Inc.

Katen, J. (1984, March 22). Car makers use "image" map as tool to position products. *Wall Street Journal*, p. 33.

Lippmann, W. (1945). *Public Opinion.* New York: Macmillan Publishing Co. Little addresses Tuscon business community leaders. (1981). *PRSA National Newsletter*, 9, (6), p. 3.

Molnar, C. (1994). Cybersex. *Adbusters*, Vol. 3, No. 1, Winter, pp. 22-23.

Nimmo, D. (1974). *Popular Images of Politics.* Englewood Cliffs: Prentice-Hall.

Perinbanayagam, R.S. (1985). *Signifying Acts: Structure and meaning in everyday life.* Carbondale: Southern Illinois University Press

Shibutani, T. (1975). Reference Groups and Social Control. *Human Behavior and Social Processes: An interactionist approach.* Edited by Arnold M.Rose. Boston: Houghton.

# Chapter 4

# Image and Public Relations

## Link between Sociodrama and Image

Sociodrama is a way to understand communication through a shared imagery expressed in some sort of drama. Images, in turn, affect how we relate to one another. It is important to discuss images in more detail for two reasons. First, they are an important concept within sociodrama; and second, they are very important to the practice of public relations. Parinbanaygan (1987) says: "Every feature that the mind creates and composes is inconceivable without their being made in terms of acts, scenes, agents, agencies, purposes, and attitudes."

An important writer from the tradition of symbolic interactionism, Charles Horton Cooley (1918) talks about images as *facts* that need to be studied in their own right, and not as something extra or superficial that we can never really know. He stresses the importance of the concept of image because it underlies both self identify and social identity. We understand both ourselves and our social organizations through the images we have of us and them. Cooley argues that we know only through images and in no other way.

Cooley also ties together the importance of looking at the communication process as symbolic interaction and the concept of image. Although he does not mention public relations, he does discuss image as a symbolic interactionist scholar. His work, therefore, has a place in any discussion of public relations theory. Cooley gives further theoretical basis for the link between sociodrama and public relations.

As the result of the discussion so far, three summary statements of sociodrama can be made. They are as follows:

1. **Communication involves the creation of dramas, through language, that involve us as participants.**

Duncan (1953) explains it this way:

> Communication as symbolic interaction between two (or more) human beings acting together is the basic human condition. The conceptual model best suited for study can be found in the drama.

## 2.  The dramas we enact in communication involve images that, in turn, govern our behavior.

In speaking and writing, we create images for ourselves and those with whom we communicate. We cannot communicate without image. Duncan (1953) refers to his mentor, Kenneth Burke:

> Burke's technique of symbolic analysis consists of codifying the 'associational clusters' in the work of a writer or speaker. The basic unit for such analysis is the **image**, not the word, sentence, paragraph, or other lexical units as such.

Foder (1979) strengthens the argument when he discusses the "representational system' that we use to make sense of even everyday things like breakfast cereal. The words we use relate to something that we all can relate to on some level. That *something* is what we call image. Foder's views are very similar to the view of image in sociodrama. He says,

> A conceptual story [read *drama*], not a casual relationship, is a philosophical approach to the relationship between eating Wheaties and its image as Breakfast of Champions. The theories of concept learning are incoherent unless they presuppose that a representational system is available to the organism.

## 3.  Sociodrama becomes clear in practice when we look at the kind of language we use when writing and speaking.

Duncan says:

> If we assume that society arises in and through communication, the study of communication becomes the study of human relations [read *public relations*]. What we can express, where, when, how, and why, the analysis of the communicative means provided for meeting situations and especially situations in which there is much ambiguity, will tell us much about how men are related.As objects and events are named, they are experienced, for names evoke the qualities of the social relation in which

they are used. We cannot act with one another or, for that matter, toward things, until we have learned the names which the society has given to such action.

When we can name things, we can relate to them. The names come from our interaction with others in the culture. The names, in turn, become expressive within the imagery of our speech or written words. We communicate through the imagery of a drama, whether in one-to-one communication or in the areas of organizational communication, public speaking, or mass media.

When we start to research and plan for public relations activity, we might look at the first step as **image-search**, an active listening for the images each audience has of our organization, product, or service. Then when we plan a public relations campaign, we can use those images to communicate with them. We know that our audiences relate to us through those images.

For example, the prevailing image you may have of a community hospital is that the staff cares about you, the patient [actor]. The setting is small and personal [scene]. They are there to serve you and make you feel comfortable [purpose]. They offer a wonderful health lecture series as a form of community education in the fall and spring [means]. They are in the business of real healthcare, not mass production, like some hospitals [act]. All the images here are clothed in the elements of a sociodrama of public relations language.

## Cooley on Image

Public relations professionals need to look seriously at the term, *image*. When we talk about public relations and image, do we mean simply that public relations puts an image in front of the public and not the *real* thing? Do we mean that public relations is concerned more with the impressions that people have rather than the truth? Public relations involves motivating people and a source for that motivation is the images that various audiences have of the organization and those within it.

Today there is much concern about the concept of image in public relations research. *The Journal of Public Relations Research* (1993) devoted an entire issue to scholarly articles on the subject. The titles of the articles in this issue included: "Image and Public Relations Practice," "A Human Nature Approach to Image and Ethics in International Public Relations," and "Images and Strategic Corporate and Marketing Planning."

Moffitt (1994) studies corporate image and uses a cultural analysis approach. The author shows that images are produced by organizational, social, and personal relations; texts; and personal experiences. Aronoff and Baskin (1983) describe the image of an organization as a component of people's attitudes and beliefs about the organization.

Lippman (1932), the journalist who had something to say about many fields of study, gave one meaning of image which is right on target for what we mean by image in sociodrama. He said,

> The only feeling that anyone can have about an event he does not experience is the feeling aroused by his mental **image** of that event. That is why until we know what others think they know, we cannot truly understand their acts.

Images can help us understand how people are motivated if we look at the image as connected with how we know something. The image is an inner representational system that enables us to relate to self and others. We see and make sense of the world around us through the images we have of it. It is from that perspective that a discussion of image can prove helpful to public relations practice.

Sociodrama places much emphasis on image as both *self-referent*, which means we learn about the individual by the kinds of images he has, and *constructive*, which means people create their own images by interacting with one another, especially through conversation.

Image must be demystified for the field of public relations. Albert Sullivan (1965), a former Boston University public relations professor, has written on the importance of the concept of image for the field of public relations. He argues that:

> Images are the proper function of public relations and warrant the most careful understanding and usage. Images are, by definition, indirect carriers of information; and in this indirectness inhere several qualities affecting external images, particularly, which are projected along the mass media.

Charles Horton Cooley (1864-1929), a pioneer in the area of symbolic interactionism and an important influence on both George Herbert Mead and Hugh Duncan, presents a systematic approach to the meaning of image.

A prevailing criticism is that images are manipulated, created, or engineered by communication professionals and forced on an unsuspect-

ing audience to elicit a positive thought for or response to the organization represented by that communication professional. Such a view of image conceals false assumptions that Cooley disputes, concerning how we
come to know what we know and how we act on our knowledge. Some
of these assumptions are: we are not free beings; others are always doing
something *to* us; our action is simply a reaction; social action is determined mainly by outside social forces. Both Cooley and the theory of
sociodrama reject these assumptions.

The assumptions stem from the belief that society is constantly in
conflict with individuals. In this view, the ultimate victor is society. With
such a view of society there can be no other view of *image* than negative.
In other words, others are manipulating us by forcing images upon us,
whether in interpersonal communication or in the mass media. Gibb (1979)
seems to buy into that theory when he says, "In most of our social intercourse someone is trying to do something to someone else - to change an
attitude, to influence behavior, or to restrict the field of activity." Is Gibb
right? He is if we look at images as something ephemeral, superficial,
and not real. He is if we see actors as determined by society rather than as
free beings who guide their own destiny.

Sociodrama theory holds that we are free and responsible actors in
our communication with one another; that we create the images we have
that guide our behavior; and that through our interactions with others we
learn the world of images that will enable us to function within a particular social order.

Can we therefore really force an image on others? We know in our
gut that we can't. Cooley, in fact, stresses that all of us, including public
relations practitioners, are faced with audiences who already have their
own set of images, which were created by them in their communication
with each other. It is this truth regarding image that becomes crucial for
the field of public relations if either students or practitioners want to view
the field from a theoretical foundation that has its roots in a humanistic
approach to human behavior. We need images to relate to one another
and we create them through the choices we make in seeking knowledge.

A discussion of image is tied into how we understand human nature,
the process of learning, and how we become motivated. Sullivan (1965)
offers some sober ground for reflection when he writes,

> Public relations has been too superficial in its thinking about information
> as an image-process. It has been satisfied too easily by its successes in
> reaching enormous numbers of people through the mass media with SOME

information; with modifying group opinions and attitudes in a generally positive direction; with specific campaigns promoting some specific
action.

In order to function in a world filled with an abundance of stimuli
each day, we make choices in response to our need for a certain order in
our lives. Images are, therefore, essentially self-referent. They begin
and serve their purpose as orienting phenomena for each individual.

Cooley, social psychologist, treats the concept of image extensively
in his book *Human Nature and the Social Order.* Rose (1962) says: "Symbolic interactionistic theory had its American origin around the turn of
the century in the writings of C. H. Cooley, John Dewey, J. M. Baldwin,
W. I. Thomas and others."

As we saw in Chapter 2, the symbolic interactionist view looks at the
human person as an actor, not as a reactor or simply one who responds to
roles indicated by society. The individual negotiates, primarily through
language, the meanings necessary for him in his everyday life. No *thing*
has meaning. Instead, the actors create the meaning in everything for themselves. Human life is a formative process and not a mere arena for the
expression of pre-existing factors.

A discussion of image within the field of public relations follows the
same line of thought. Images are necessary to relate to one another. We
create the ones we need. We give meaning to experience through which
we create and reinforce images of organizations, people, events, etc. An
image, therefore, has a history connected with it: past, present, and fu-
ture.

Cooley's major contributions to the field of sociology are the concepts of organic society, social self, primary group, and communication.
He was not the only one at the beginning of this century to talk about
these concepts, nor was he the last, but his works are devoted to an extensive analysis of them. Most of these concepts have been developed extensively by other social scientists since Cooley. It is, however, Cooley's
discussion of the term *image* as underlying these familiar concepts that
sets him apart and makes him so important for our discussion of
sociodrama.

What we see as we look at each of these concepts is *imagination*.
Image, or imagination, are key words in Cooley's work. He wrote that,
"The imaginations which people have of one another are the solid facts of
society, and that to observe and interpret these must be a chief aim of
sociology."

Cooley's entire premise might be phrased in this way: in studying organic society, primary group, the social self, and communication, we need to study the image. To study human behavior we need to understand images and see the search as understanding human motivation. We need to look at the *image* of being together, the group experience, the self, our own communication, and what that image means for the individual. As a result, we come to better understand ourselves and the organization we represent.

Philanthropy, for instance, cannot be understood without thinking about what images the giver and recipient have of each other. "In other words, we want to get at motives, and motives spring from personal ideas," says Cooley (1918). Cooley recognized that focusing on image or imagination was not new, but that serious thought must be given to it and that professionals must view it as a valid field of social science study. Sociodrama gives strong focus to the images that we use to relate to one another. Image is studied because it is an important field of inquiry in its own right. The field of public relations should be less apologetic about the word *image*.

For Cooley, individuals and society must be studied primarily as they are imagined since we know only through images. A public relations practitioner is interested in what image the audience has in regard to an organization and its product or service. That is a crucial point of reference. Cooley (1918) explains that, "It is surely true, prima facie, that the best way of observing things is that which is most direct; and I do not see how any one can hold that we know persons directly except as imaginative ideas in the mind."

## a. Organic Society and Image

Society, according to Cooley, is an organic whole held together by the imagination of each member of that whole. He says,

> If we take society to include the whole of human life, this may truly be said to be organic, in the sense that influences may be and are transmitted from one part to any other part, so that all parts are bound together into an interdependent whole.

All of life, for humans, is unified by interaction. Each phase of it must be and is, in some degree, an expression of the whole system. By experiencing a part of the society, we have an image of the whole of society. That is what gives meaning to our individual experience.

This organic whole, or society, is the combined total of images that all its members have. Society is imagined and thus becomes what it is for its members. Cooley says:

> Each man's imagination, regarded as a mass of personal impressions worked up into a living, growing whole, is a special phase of society; and Mind or Imagination as a whole, that is human thought considered in the largest way as having a growth and organization extending throughout the ages, is the LOCUS of society in the widest possible sense.

Each member of a society knows others through images. Cooley says,

> The idea of a person, whether his body be present to our senses or not, is imaginative, a synthesis, an interpretation of many elements, resting upon our whole experience of human life, not merely upon our acquaintance with this particular person.

We think of one another in terms of the images we have of each other. We interpret others so that we can make sense of one another, and that interpretation is the action of a compilation of images which enables us to relate to a particular individual or organization.

Through his discussion of society as an organic entity, Cooley describes the imagination as the place in which society exists. Though we are separated from one another, we are part of the whole in the imagination. The impact of images is to hold society together. Images are created in interaction and at the same time reinforced by interaction.

The janitor in my company and my client both have images of the organization. Both of the images are real because they both motivate the individual to deal with the organization in a particular way. To know the images is to know how the organization is functioning. The organization is only as real as its images in the minds of the people with whom it deals.

## b.  Primary Group and Image

In his discussion of primary groups, Cooley gives special emphasis to the concept of image. He defines primary groups as follows:

> By primary groups I mean those characterized by intimate face-to-face association and cooperation. They are primary in several senses, but chiefly in that they are fundamental in forming the social nature and ide-

als of the individual. The result of intimate association, psychologically, is a certain fusion of individualities in a common whole, so that one's very self, for many purposes at least, is the common life and purpose of the group.

Human nature is not something existing separately in the individual, but a group-nature or primary phase of society, a relatively simple and general condition of the social mind. To highlight the influence on imagination from the primary group, Cooley says:

> The social person is a group of sentiments attached to some symbol or other characteristic element, which keeps them together and from which the whole idea is named... The social and moral reality is that which lives in our imaginations and affects our motives.

We obtain images of group life from the symbols that are important to us. We use the symbol as a link to the group. *To know the symbols that people use to relate to each other is to know the images that people have of one another.* That is the groundwork of sociodrama.

George Herbert Mead (1964) writes of the concept of image and the primary group in his essay on Cooley:

> If an individual consists of the ideas in his mind which he imagines that others entertain of him, and if the others exist as members of society as the ideas which he entertains in his imagination, it is evident that they will have common goods insofar as they are organized in his imagination into some social whole, such as a family.

The primary group gives an individual his/her support system. In a primary group, one can discuss one's hopes and dreams and feel a sense of acceptance. Whether the primary group is found in the home, at work, on the playground, or in the neighborhood, Cooley says that the influence of the group is through the images the individual carries around about the members of the group. The individual imagines what others imagine of him, and this becomes the groundwork from which he constructs his own identity. O.J. Simpson was so terrified of events souring his image among his fans that he almost committed suicide.

To understand the images that others have of us, as individuals or as corporations, is to understand how others act toward us and how to understand ourselves. This thought from Cooley is quite appropriate for understanding sociodrama as the way we relate to self and others. We enact dramas in our imagination through our speaking and writing. We don't simply relate, we relate through dialogue, expressed as drama.

## c.   Social Self and Image

Another important concept for Cooley is *social self*. According to him, self and society are *twin-born*. He writes that to separate the two in discussion is a waste of time.

In keeping with his central concept of image, Cooley says that we develop a self through our imagining of what others think of us. It is important for both individuals and institutions to know what images others have of them, because those images become the path to self-understanding. He says,

"Nevertheless this highest self is a social self, in that it is a product of constructive imagination working with the materials which social experience supplies. Our ideals of personal character are built up out of thoughts and sentiments developed by intercourse, and very largely by imagining how ourselves would appear in the minds of persons we look up to. These are not necessarily living persons; any one that is at all real, that is imaginable, to us, becomes a possible occasion of social self-feeling."

## d.   Communication and Image

Finally, Cooley looks at the concept of *communication*. It is through communication, especially language, that we create our imagination. Cooley writes:

"By communication is here meant the mechanism through which human relations exist and develop - all the symbols of the mind, together with the means of conveying them through space and preserving them in time. It includes the expression of the face, attitude and gesture, the tones of the voice, words, writing, printing, railways, telegraphs, telephones, and whatever else may be the latest achievement in the conquest of space and time."

Communication is interaction through symbol. The interaction is two-way because there are at least two people involved in the process. It is communication that creates the mind and, in turn, the mind which creates communication. Cooley explains,

If we take a larger view and consider the life of a social group, we see that communication, including the organization into literature, art, and institutions, is truly the outside or visible structure of thought as much cause as effect of the inside or conscious life of men.

Images work on images. Images are brought to every experience and in every experience new images are produced according to the needs of the individual or group of individuals. Images are what we use to learn about ourselves, our families, our world, and our organizations. To know the origin and motivating power of these images, as Cooley shows, is to begin to construct a theory of public relations, whose focus is *images*. Such a theory is **sociodrama**.

Images are the means whereby the audiences of public relations guide their activity. We cannot push an image into the audience member like rolling a ball down a bowling alley because she/he produces her own image *according to her needs*. People create their own images by interacting with one another. That is the meaning that Cooley gives to the term image or imagination.

We are co-creators of the world in which we live. Our images guide our behavior in that world. As Cooley says, "The imaginations which people have of one another are the solid facts of society."

Public relations practitioners need to do research in order to understand what images a particular public has of a product, a company, or a service they represent. Communication planning needs to be built on that research so that the audience will be able to understand and be motivated in response to the public relations issue. This research is not simply market research but **image research** and cannot be tackled simply by a survey. More qualitative research methods are needed in order to listen to the audience or group involved. People, as Cooley argues, construct their own images through how they interact with others, particularly in their imaginations. Who better to tell us about that image than the member of the audience?

Sociodrama points to the importance of images for understanding how both the internal and external audiences relate to an organization. Images are organizational maps that make sense of daily experience. We use the images we have produced for our own needs. How do we understand the images that the audiences have of the organization? The images can be traced on an image-search grid, which is used in the sociodrama model for planning public relations activity.

# Looking for Images in Sociodrama:
# The Image-Search Grid

The MacCannells (1982) in their book on signs say:

> All cultural systems (religions, languages, normatively governed face-to-face behavior, etc.) project unified imagery that attracts support in the form of faith or belief. This imagery is the domain of general semiotic research.

Fiol (1989) discusses semiotics as a way to understand an organization's imagery. While letters to shareholders directly communicate facts about a firm, they also communicate implicit beliefs about the organization and its relationships with the surrounding world. A semiotic method of textual analysis was used to analyze the narratives in the language of the letters. The narratives embody the images the organizational leadership has. The study discusses the link between language and image. The language reveals the imagery of the organization's leadership rather than becoming a tool for communication by presenting facts to the shareholder audience. Perhaps, the organization needed to learn the images held by the audience.

In order to visualize the discussion of image and the sociodrama theory, we return to the grid which was first introduced in Chapter 2 [See Figure 1, next page].

The purpose of the Image-Search Grid is to offer a visual tool for both understanding and researching the images surrounding a particular issue, organization, idea, service, or product. The Grid is a matrix of rows and columns which represent the elements and the levels of the drama in sociodrama. With this grid, the **levels** of the drama are shown along the top and the **elements** of the drama are listed down the left side.

As the levels and elements meet, they create cells (e.g., 1a, 1b, 1c). These cells indicate a relationship between a level and an element within that level. For example, the cell where **act** and **behind-the-scenes** meet refers to the image that focuses on what is going on (act) in the office or organization (behind the scenes).

To use the grid, we need to listen to how people talk or write about the organization, placing their value statements (not factual statements) in the most appropriate cells on the matrix. The method of listening to others can include individual or group interviews or analysis of written stories, brochures, newsletters, etc.

Figure 1:

## SOCIODRAMA GRID

*Levels of the Drama*

| Elements of the Drama | a. Behind-the-scenes | b. On Stage | c. Outside the Theater |
|---|---|---|---|
| 1. act | 1a | 1b | 1c |
| 2. scene | 2a | 2b | 2c |
| 3. means | 3a | 3b | 3c |
| 4. actors | 4a | 4b | 4c |
| 5. purpose | 5a | 5b | 5c |

Remember that the way that people talk about our organization is in dramatic metaphors. They don't just say the organization is "good" or "bad." They load their statements with value judgements and feelings. It is in those terms that people imagine the organization and therefore relate to it.

A nurse, an employee of a particular hospital, might say: "This hospital is just out to make as much money as possible; they don't care about health care." That is the image of a particular actor. Her image is filled with value statements and judgements. It is not a factual statement that all people would agree with. What is important is that the statement represents the drama in which this person perceives the organization. The imagery, as expressed in her words, can be placed in one or more of the cells on the Grid.

For example, the statement: "This hospital is just out to make as much money as possible," could be put in cell 5a, which is where **purpose** and **behind-the-scenes** form a relationship. Her image of the purpose of the hospital, according to those who make the decisions (the Board and the administrators who are behind the scenes) is that the hospital simply wants to make money. The statement, "They don't care about health care" could be put in cell 4a, which is **actors** and **behind-the-scenes**. In this case, her image of the leaders of the hospital is that they make decisions that indicate they are not really concerned about health care.

To show that our images tend to be consistent with the way we look at the world, that same nurse might also say: "The nurses are the key to a well-run hospital. What the patient remembers is the care from the nurse." That would be a statement for cell 4b. The nurse's image of the patient is that he/she comes primarily for good care from the nurses. That image of the hospital certainly defends her position as a nurse and, at the same time, does not conflict with her negative image of hospital leadership. She sees the hospital moving away from good patient care with its concern for bringing in revenue.

What is at issue here is not what is true or false, but rather in what ways people imagine the organization. This is the image of a particular nurse at a particular hospital. What is important for public relations (in this case, internal public relations) is that others probably share that view given the fact that we create our imagery especially through talking to others.

A person will have images of the organization or product or service and express them in terms of the elements and the levels of a drama. As we have seen earlier, images are the way we relate to each other, particularly in our conversations with each other. A hospital is not simply "good" or "bad." It is, rather, "Good as far as I'm concerned!" or "For me, it's a no-win situation!." We always make judgements in terms of our own way of looking at the world, but when we express it, we choose words that will paint a picture of what we mean: tones, colors, heroes, victims, timing, pace.

An earlier discussion of image described an organization as a mosaic of similar and conflicting images. Actors within the audiences of an organization can have opposing views of the same organization. The finance director of the same hospital might, for example, say, "This hospital is finally serving the community and staying out of the red!" His image would be placed in cell 1b where **act** and **on-stage** form a relationship. His meaning is that the hospital is doing what it is supposed to do, i.e. serve the community and survive financially. This image certainly contradicts that of the nurse, yet both are an important public or audience view of the same hospital. Both see the hospital from the view of the image each needs to function well and feel good about himself/herself in that world. They do not see the same hospital. They see a piece of the mosaic, or one image, that is important to them. They relate to the hospital through their image of that organization.

Treadwell (1993) says that it is more accurate to think not of an organizational image, but of a diversity of images which are explained by the backgrounds, attitudes, and communication experiences of the individuals that have contact with the organization. It is helpful to regard image as a multi-faceted, idiosyncratic receiver perspective on an organization and to draw a distinction between image and organization identity which is the organization's *desired* or *paradigmatic* image.

In public relations practice it is important to recognize that the publics share different, and sometimes contradictory, images. It might be tempting to say they do not *really* know or understand the hospital. Such a statement misses the mark. They only know what they imagine the hospital to be for them. No matter what the desired or paradigmatic image the hospital may want them to hold out, that knowing is all they have. In their day-to-day relationship with the hospital it is that image which they see.

When the nurse is at the supermarket, for example, and she meets an old friend who asks her about the hospital, she might say something like this: "It's all money. All they want to do today in healthcare is to make sure the books balance." She talks about the organization in terms of her image of it. Notice the colorful words, "money" and "balancing the books," which express her imagery of the hospital in a dramatic way.

The Image-Search Grid helps put flesh on the theory of sociodrama by allowing us to locate the various kinds of value and opinion statements people make about an organization and its product or service. Such statements ultimately help us visualize the predominant images held by the various audiences.

As professionals, when we understand the prevailing images, we are in a position to plan effective public relations activity.

# References

Aronoff, C.E. and Baskin, O.W. (1983). *Public Relations: The profession and the practice.* St. Paul, MN: West Publishing, Co.

Cooley, C.H. (1902). *Human nature and the social order.* New York: C. Scribner's Sons.

Cooley C.H. (1918). *Social process.* New York: C. Scribner's Sons.

Duncan, H. (1953). *Language & Literature in society.* Bedminster Press.

Fiol, C. Marlene. (1989). *A semiotic analysis of corporate language: Organizational boundaries and joint venturing.* Administrative Science Quarterly, 34, No. 2, pp. 277-303.

Foder, J.A. (1979). *Language of thought.* Cambridge, MA: Harvard University Press.

Gibb, J.R. (1979). Defensive communication. In C.D. Mortensen (Ed.), *Basic readings in communication theory* (2nd ed.). New York: Harper & Row.

Journal of Public Relations Research. Volume 5, 3, 1993.

Lippman, W. (1992). *Public opinion.* New York: Harcourt, Brace & Co.

MacCannell, D. and MacCannell, J.F. (1987). *The time of the sign: Semiotic interpretation of modern culture.* Bloomington: Indiana University Press.

Mead, G.H. (1964). *The social psychology of George Herbert Mead.* Chicago: University of Chicago Press.

Moffitt, M.A. (1994). *A cultural studies perspective toward understanding corporate image: A case study of State Farm Insurance.* Journal of Public Relations Research. Vol 6, N.1, p. 23-67.

Perinbanayagam, R.S. (1987). Drama in Everyday Life. *Studies in Symbolic Interaction*, edited by Norman K. Denzin, Greenwich, CT: JAI Press, 8, p. 121-141.

Rose, A.M. (1962). A systematic summary of symbolic interaction theory. In A.M. Rose (Ed.), *Human behavior and social processes: An interactionist approach.* Boston: Hougton Mifflin Co.

Sullivan, A.J. (1965). *Toward a philosophy of public relations: Images in public relations.* In O. Lerbinger & A. Sullivan (Eds.), Information, influence & communication: A reader in public relations. New York: Basic Books.

Treadwell, D.F. (1993). *What image? Assessing the subtleties of image of a non-profit organization.* Paper presented to the International Communication Association.

# Chapter 5

# Method for Sociodrama Research

## A Question of What Kind of Method

The goal of sociodrama is to understand public relations as interaction rather than as simply sending out messages to a target audience. In sociodrama we have seen the importance of images that both the organization and the audiences have. Images, according to Cooley, are the *facts of society*. People arrive at their images primarily in conversation with others whom they trust.

Researching images as portrayed through sociodrama requires an understanding of how people *image* a company, product, or service. In other words, we have to allow people a chance to talk about it and listen to their discourse.

It does little good to talk about the importance of the image without having some guidance on how to do the necessary research on images. Several methods frequently presented as social science research methods include surveys and content analysis. Such methods frequently assume that there is an hypothesis to be tested or, at least, an objective to be measured.

In sociodrama and the search for the images for the practice of public relations, we are not concerned so much with testing a hypothesis as with *understanding* our publics or audience. Hypothesis testing, which is closely aligned with prediction and control, is more aligned to the one-way transmission model of communication in many public relations texts on the subject. The sociodrama model of public relations, in moving away from a positivist perspective, calls for an alternative method of researching an audience that is more cultural, ethnographic, and interpretive.

A research method for sociodrama is needed to reveal relationships and the development of images for individuals or audiences. Most *objective* reseachers already have an idea what they will find and, not too amazingly, often find out what they set out to prove. Such is the case with much of the research conducted through surveys and even content analysis.

Moffitt (1992) proposes that public relations research allign itself with cultural studies in order to look at the notions of *meaning* and *audience*, which, in turn, inform the public relations concept of public. She proposes ethnography, a qualitative and subjective approach.

Sociodrama needs such a subjective method of research in which the subjects are allowed to express themselves *in their own words*. Because we are looking for personal images, a research method is needed that will encourage people to talk about what *they*, and not the researcher, feel is important. The use of unstructured, open-ended interviewing and discussion is the first step. Two research methods prove to be most effective for sociodrama: focus interviews and Q methodology.

## Focus Interviews

The focus group interview is used commonly in communication and marketing research. Grunig (1993) also uses focus interviews in public relations to study image and symbolic leadership. The focus interview, an in-depth interview with one or more persons, may last at least thirty minutes and can go as long as two hours. It is conducted with a group of about five to twelve persons who discuss their own perceptions, feelings, attitudes, and opinions about a particular issue. The group is led by a skilled leader who lets the topic of the conversation develop. The leader does not manipulate the group or lead it to affirm what he or the client wants to hear. The individuals in the group are allowed the opportunity to express how they feel about a particular topic (Krueger).

A fundamentally important requirement in focus interviews is that members of the group must adequately represent the population to be studied. A careful selection process is important in choosing the subjects so they reflect the general demographics of the subject population.

The leader of the group will prepare a list of questions to ask or issues to bring up so that the group has a focus. *Focus* simply means that the group will center their discussion around a certain issue by talking about their feelings and perceptions of that issue. It is a good idea to select a group of people who feel strongly about an issue in differing ways. The discussion may raise feelings in some members of the group who will speak about the issue only when they hear an opinion that opposes theirs. Members of focus interview groups should to be able to

verbalize their feelings. They should also be present voluntarily to ensure their cooperation in the process.

The Image-Search Grid discussed in Chapter 4 can serve as a guide
for the preparation of the questions. It is a good idea to ask questions that
will allow the subjects to discuss the issue in terms of the elements and
the levels of the drama. Remember we are looking for the kind of images
they have and images, according to sociodrama, are expressed in terms of
a drama. As we have seen in Axiom #5:

> ### *We relate to each other through written or spoken words that have the characteristics of drama.*

For example, we are interested in knowing the community image of
ABC Company. The company is thinking of doing some community
service for the local town, but in this tight economic environment the
company does not know what to do. Should they contribute to the local
library fund, support community theater, or help restore a local park?
One might begin by phrasing a question with a group of neighbors of the
company in this way: "What does ABC do?" (lb, **act** and **on-stage**). Or,
"What does the general community think of the company's facility?" (5c,
**purpose** and **outside-the-theater**). In each of these questions, the subjects in the group have an opportunity to talk about the company in terms
of dramatic metaphors.

Although the subjects are talking about how they perceive the company and how they perceive what others feel about it, they are basically
talking about themselves and their image of the company. Any discussion of feelings — no matter what issue it relates to — is basically self-
referent (about ourselves). That is an important point in looking at public
relations as sociodrama. We look at the world as it relates to us, and by
our conversations we justify our way of looking at the world. Axiom #1
stated:

> ### *Language is a way of explaining and a way of creating motives that lead to a certain kind of action.*

The group leader ought to prepare a series of fifteen questions each
based on the fifteen cells of the Image-Search Grid. If the members of
the focus interview group discuss an issue before it shows up on the pre-
pared list, the leader can simply skip to that question and go back to the
others when appropriate.

Since sociodrama requires subjective research, it is important to listen to the interviewees express themselves and the way they look at the world. Their images will become clearer to those conducting the research if they are allowed to talk and elaborate. A leader provides a framework for discussion, and therefore cannot add his/her own images to the discussion during the interview,

Since focus groups are conducted purposively, the data collected from them needs to be recorded in some way. As is the case with most qualitative research, in focus group research the major issues brought up by the subjects become the data. In this research it is not a question of three people bringing up a certain topic, but rather that the group had the opportunity to respond to the issue because it was brought up by the group in the first place. What we think is important may not be so once people in the group have had a chance to discuss it and look at it according to their perceptions. Frequent phrases, common themes, and similar descriptions are what the researcher is interested in from focus group interviews. Focus interviews should be recorded with either audio or videotape to ensure accurate data-gathering.

The subjects identify with the organization in some way and have images of the company because of that identification. People have an image of the president of the company, the manager, the sales people, and what the company does. It is not a question of fact or factual data, but rather what is important to them in terms of the organization. Axiom #7 of sociodrama explains:

*In public relations we create sociodramas which have a certain built-in hierarchy and with which the organization and the public identify.*

The data-gathering procedure seeks to understand the subjects' sociodrama through the descriptions, stories, examples, etc. that embody their images on certain issues. The public relations of the organization is present in that discourse.

## Q Sorting

The goal of any research in sociodrama is to understand the subjective world of the actor or subject. The first step is conducting focus interviews. Second, we begin to look for the themes, patterns, or images in more detail, through a research methodology called *Q sorting*, which will use the material from the focus interviews. Maudlin (1985) defines Q in this way: "Simply stated, Q is an instrument, like a camera, for taking pictures of subjectivity. It is a tool for producing physical evidence of the content, structure, and dynamics of subjectivity."

The concept of Q was developed by psychologist William Stephenson in the 1930's. His works have touched various aspects of human behavior such as communication, marketing, and public opinion. Stephenson (1953) recommends using Q or Q sorting to ascertain the public image of an organization, because imagery is what creates feelings about a person, idea, product, or institution in relation to one's own ego or self-involving motives. He provides a method for what Boulding, Nimmo, and Duncan have discussed more theoretically.

Levy (1990), a researcher in advertising, says:

> My clients attempt to develop businesses by fabricating their products and services and crafting advertising messages to the needs and wants of particular segments. The Q sort is my principle method for understanding the beliefs, opinions, and attitudes of consumers. I am constantly amazed with each study I do in the variation of people's views on the products they buy."

We want to understand the images a person holds of a company or organization. His image of it is related to how he sees himself and what the company or organization does to satisfy the needs of his ego. Images are integrally connected to how each person identifies himself with the organization in dramatic metaphors. But those images are identified with others who also connect in some way with the organization. As Cooley pointed out, our common images are what connect us with our community.

One person may meet friends at a local McDonald's. For that person, McDonald's portrays the image of *friend*. Another person saves time by eating at that same fast food establishment. For that person, McDonald's portrays the image of *helper*.

Stephenson (1963) says: "An important concept in communication research, stemming chiefly from advertising research, is image—meaning conceptions of and associations with products or ideas, usually of a dynamic nature."

Q is a way to look at the images that guide the behavior of the various subjects or audiences which maintain a relationship to a particular company or organization.

The actual process of Q sorting is the catagorizing of a group of statements or pictures by a subject. For example, a public relations practitioner wants to research the public image of ABC, Inc. Using a Q sort procedure, a subject or a group of subjects sorts a set of short written statements about the organization or about any issue within it, like the image of the newsletter or the annual report or company policy. The statements are the predominant themes from the focus group interviews which were conducted previously with other subjects. This sorting, which serves to rank order each statement, leads to the creation of an image or images through correlation and factor analysis.

Treadwell (1993) sees Q methodology helpful in understanding organizational image for the practice of public relations. Image should be seen in terms of the multidimensional idiosyncratic approach taken by Crable and Vibbert (1986) who define image as a personally-believed mental picture that is descriptive, evaluative, and predisposing in relation to some object.

The focus of Q is discovering what kinds of images people have. The issue is not, as in a public opinion poll, that an attitude is held by a certain percentage of the public. Q is concerned with personal, subjective meanings. In Q individuals use statements to model their own conceptions, thereby revealing their own frame of reference. They create their own images by the way they interpret the written statements. They say to themselves as they read a statement, "Does this statement mean this, or that, to me?" or "This statement is definitely one about which I feel quite strongly."

Maudlin (1985), who uses Q extensively, says,

> Learning the technical process for doing Q studies, including the statistical underpinnings, is not a trivial pursuit for most, but neither is it out of reach for normally, bright, diligent persons.

> However, one of the difficulties, and thus one of the weaknesses of Q is that it emphasizes the most difficult-to-teach research skills—focused interviewing, construction of projective materials for the research instrument (the sort), development of penetrating conditions of instruction (in studies that use multiple conditions of instruction), interpretation of 'subjective' evidence, and application of the interpretation.

The statements used in the Q-sort process represent what an audience, not the researcher, thinks is important. That is the basis of what one might call **Image-Search** for sociodrama, making it an appropriate methodology for understanding others and how they motivate themselves toward an organization. Image-Search, the umbrella term for the primary research method for sociodrama, aligns itself with the more humanistic tradition of understanding human behavior based on symbolic interaction.

It is important that a Q statement be a self-referent statement that you cannot prove or disprove. It also must be very clear and concise. The subject must understand what a statement means immediately. The statements ought to represent dominant themes in the interviews and are selected in such a way that each of the statements relates to one of the five elements and three levels of the drama as closely as possible.

For example, in Table 1 there are 48 statements that come directly from focus interviews. The statements are phrased directly from the interviews, and only grammatical changes are made to them. In a case where several people say the same thing, the statement that is easiest to understand is chosen. Each of the 48 statements fit into the fifteen cells of the Image-Search Grid.

Table 2 exhibits the set of instructions given to subjects involved in Q sorting. Note that they are asked to sort the statements according to a certain frame of reference. For example, they are asked to "sort [the statements] as they represent your feelings about the company." This is called the *condition of instruction*, as referred to by Maudlin.

Table 3 shows a score sheet with a grid for recording the number of the statement, along with a space for a few questions about the subject. A score is given for each of the 48 items on the basis of a forced quasi-normal frequency distribution. The subjects look at each statement and assign it a number from, and possibly including, a -5 to a +5 depending on their feeling for or opinion of that statement. In the grid exhibited in Table 3, there are eight spaces to record statements that score a "0." These eight in the middle are the largest pile in the sort. Stephenson designed Q sorting on the basis that most people have highly positive or negative feelings about only a few things in life. People generally do not care about or do not know enough about the majority of the statements provided, and therefore do not exhibit strong positive or negative feelings about them. Stephenson suggests that the larger number of statements be relegated to the area closer to the center (-1, 0, +1). Q is primarily interested in what subjects feel strongly about, as shown by a -5 or +5 on the score sheet.

The sorting takes an individual about 30 minutes and can be administered in person or even through the mail. The subjects weigh the meaning and value of each statement against the others. The statements hold

Table 1

The numbers in the cells represent the statements which were
derived from the focus interviews.

## SOCIODRAMA GRID

*Levels  of  the  Drama*

| *Elements of the Drama* | a. Behind the scenes | b. On Stage | c. Outside the Theater |
|---|---|---|---|
| 1. act | 14, 28, 48 | 13, 43, 45 | 33, 36, 40 |
| 2. scene | 3, 10, 17, 21 | 29, 37, 47 | 2, 24, 34 |
| 3. means | 5, 20, 31, 41 | 7, 25, 30 | 18, 22, 23 |
| 4. actors | 1, 8, 15 | 12, 27, 39 | 35, 38, 42 |
| 5. purpose | 4, 6, 9 | 11, 16, 19, 26 | 32, 44, 46 |

different meanings for each subject. What emerges is a broad picture or
image of how the subject views the issue.

Talbot (1971) says:

> In the Q-factor analysis, instead of correlating columns in the matrix, you
> would correlate rows or persons and factor out clusters or groupings of
> persons. You would be concerned with the way people order items and
> with grouping them into clusters of people who order items in similar

## Table 2
### Score Sheet

Name _____

N=48

| | (Negative) | | | | | (Neutral) | | | | (Positive) | |
|---|---|---|---|---|---|---|---|---|---|---|---|
| X= | -5 | -4 | -3 | -2 | -1 | 0 | +1 | +2 | +3 | +4 | +5 |
| F= | 2 | 3 | 4 | 5 | 6 | 8 | 6 | 5 | 4 | 3 | 2 |

ways. Each group of persons would be associated with a distinctive common ordering of the items.

What is critically important is that the group of individuals participating in the sorting truly represent the group being studied. The number could be 10, 20, or 100. They share a common image as they sort like others. We are interested in the images held by various groups. Subjects invariably allign themselves with an image shared by other subjects.

Brown (1980) says:

Fundamentally, Q methodology is of utility in penetrating a situation in which the self is intimately involved, whether in political or other matters. It is therefore pertinent in the study of public opinion and attitudes, groups, roles, culture, socialization, decision making, personality, propaganda, values, communication, literature, *imagery*, and other self-involving domains—i.e. in virtually all areas of concern to the social and political sciences. Where individuals are involved and can be expected to entertain viewpoints with respect to things going on around them, however subjective these viewpoints may be, Q technique and its methodology can illuminate in broad outline the major effects that are operating.

For a more in-depth treatment of Q methodology, please refer to William Stephenson's *The Study of Subjectivity* or Stephen Brown's *Political Subjectivity*.

<u>Table 3</u>
**Instructions**

*Background Information:*

You are asked to use the statements (found on the 48 slips of paper) to represent what matters most to you, positively or negatively. Use the statements to describe your "opinion" or your "position," or "views" about the substance of the statements. Those that you feel strongly about, or that you value most positively, are given score +5. Those you feel strongly about, but negatively, are given score -5. Those statements about which you have no feelings, or about which you are neutral, score at or near zero (0). If you do not know what a statement means, it should be scored 0.

*Method: Three Piles First*

First shuffle the pack of 48 statements to randomize them. Then as you read the statements, sort them into three piles, one on the right for "pro" statements (those which provoke positive reaction in some degree), one on the left for "con" statements (those which provoke negative reaction in some degree), and one in the middle for the neutral, doubtful, ambiguous, or meaningless statements. There should be about the same number of statements in each pile.

### To-and-Fro Sorting:

Look at your Score Sheet and note the scale at the top of it: -5 through +5. As you proceed with the instructions, imagine a large score sheet in front of you with the same numbers on it.

Choose the 2 statements from the "pro" pile with which you are most strongly in agreement (i.e., about which you feel most positive). Place these face up in the position in which you intend to record them — at the far right (in +5 cells). Then choose the 2 statements from the "con" pile with which you most strongly disagree (i.e., about which you feel most negative). Place these face up in the position in which you intend to record them — at the far left (in -5 cells).

Move back to the "pro" pile and choose 3 statements with which you are next most in agreement. Place these in the position in which you intend to record them — at the right (in +4 cells). Then move to the "con" pile and choose the 3 statements with which you are next most in disagreement. Place these in the position in which you intend to record them — at the left (in -4 cells).

Continue in this manner, alternating from right to left as you approach the middle of the scale. When finished, all 48 statements should be placed in front of you. You can still change the position of any statement if you so wish. The object is to have the statements placed in the position that represents your "opinion" or "view." The above to-and-fro method is recommended as most practical and reliable, but you can do it any way you like.

### Scoring:

Record each statement's number on the Score Sheet, in the appropriate cell which indicates the score it received. Record only one number in each box. (A separate Score Sheet is provided.)

# References

Brown, S.R. (1980). *Political subjectivity: Application of a Q methodology in political science*. New Haven: Yale University Press.

Crable, R.E. and Vibbert, S.L. (1986). Public relations as communication management. Edina, MN: Bellweather Press.

Grunig, L.A. (1993). *Image and symbolic leadership: Using focus group research to bridge the gap*. Journal of Public Relations Research. Vol. 5, No. 2.

Krueger, R. A. (1988). *Focus Groups: A practical guide for applied research*. Newbury Park, CA: Sage.

Levy, D. (1990). *In Memoriam, William Stephenson, 1902-1989*. Operant Subjectivity. Vol. 13, #2, pp. 65-66.

Maudlin, C.R. (1985). *Q-method, operancy and the nature of scientific study of subjectivity*. Paper presented at the First Annual Q Conference, Columbia, MO.

Moffitt, M.A. (1992). *Bringing critical theory and ethical considerations to definitions of a "public."* Public Relations Review, 18(1): 17-29.

Morgan, D.L. (1988). *Focus Groups as qualitative research*. Newbury Park, CA: Sage.

Stephenson, W. (1953). *The study of behavior: Q-Technique and its methodology*. Chicago: University of Chicago Press.

Stephenson, W. (1963). Public images of public utilities. *Journal of advertising research*, 3, (4), 34-39.

Stephenson, W. (1967). *The play theory of mass communication*. Chicago: University of Chicago Press.

Talbott, A.D. (1971). *Q technique and it's methodology: A brief introduction and consideration*. Paper presented to the American Educational Research Association, New York.

Treadwell, D.F. (1993). *What image? Assessing the subtleties of image of a non-profit organization*. Paper presented to the International Communication Association.

# Chapter 6

# Sociodrama: Case Studies

## Introduction

The cases presented in this chapter are examples on the part of organizations or individuals to influence public opinion. Some of the cases are contemporary; some are not. Each of them accomplished a degree of success in its efforts. The primary focus of this chapter is to look at the sociodrama within each case as expressed in either written or spoken language. Axiom #4 is:

> *Sociodrama is not concerned with how society persuades us, but how words about society persuade us to act in certain ways in our social relationships.*

In each case study we look at the facts of a particular case: what the problem was; how it was handled; and what effect resulted. In hindsight we can talk about what happened by using the language of sociodrama. We ask ourselves, "How successful were they in achieving their goals?" and "How might we have done things differently were we in the same position?"

Sociodrama is one way to understand and practice public relations. The theory needs to be applied to real public relations situations. Therefore, this chapter gives the reader an opportunity to look at specific cases and see how the theory can be applied. Ways to understand a particular case from the perspective of sociodrama will be discussed.

Each case will be divided into four sections:

1. Background
2. Problem
3. Solution
4. Commentary

## Case #1:  Disneyland

### *Background*

Customer service is the important ingredient today for most businesses. Because much of our manufacturing is now being done overseas, the U.S. is becoming a service-oriented nation. The Walt Disney World theme park in Lake Buena Vista, Florida had to face the issue that visitors would expect service above all else.

### *Problem*

Disney World management was looking for a method of training their employees to deal with their customers or clients. They wanted visitors to Disney World to have a good time when they came. Disney wanted visitors to identify with the park, tell their family and friends about the experience, and return again. The management team at Disney World had to come up with language or words to enable their employees to provide good service and enable the visitors to feel part of the organization. This was a public relations problem, although the personnel and customer relations offices would do the work (at times the tasks of these three areas can overlap in any organization).

### *Solution*

A *guest courtesy* program was created for the employees.  Lasting a half-day, it trains new employees to make visitors feel at *home*. Every issue of the company newspaper talks about some aspect of the service mission. Deede Sharp (Zemke), manager of educational program development at Disney World says, "Training starts with our culture. Our first task is to make new employees partners in the corporate culture.  And the culture is focused on one thing:  making sure our guests have an enjoyable experience."

The Disney culture has two focal points:  customers are called "guests" and employees are referred to as "cast members." The cast members (employees) are trained to treat guests (customers) the way they would want to be treated. Sue Rye (Zemke), manager of human resource development for Disney World's administration/support division, says, "We make a very real effort to help employees see that they are in show business and that our job is to create a fantasy and have a role to play that has to be picture perfect. Sweeping up after the horses on Main Street isn't a fun job. We work hard at making sure the employee knows it's an important job and one that is respected and appreciated."

Again Sharp says, "We tell our people that they are cast members playing a role in a show. And like any actor, they can walk away from that role at the end of the day. Even the most upset guest is only attacking the role the employee plays, not the employee."

A stress reducer at Disney World is *job rotation*. Customer-contact people are encouraged to learn multiple roles and are provided with formal cross-training.

## Commentary

Notice the language that the public relations staff uses to create and influence the behavior of the employees. They call the employees *cast members*, thereby giving them a sense of drama together with management. They tell the employees that they are playing a role in a show. When they go home, they can leave that role behind them.

Management emphasizes that their employees are in show business, providing entertainment for their guests (customers). The employee newsletter speaks of service. The management team and the employees are referred to as a culture, a way of life. They create their culture together.

The language indicates a drama of a certain kind of social order in which both the employees and the visitors play particular roles. They identify with one another and both parties' needs are met: the visitor gets good service and the employee gets a sense of performing in a giant show.

The metaphors used in employee training are not just words, but the means of creating a culture. The language used by Deede Sharp and Sue Rye also indicate that there is a sociodrama going on in this organization, a drama in which both the management/employees and guests play certain roles so that the Disney culture can continue to exist and entertain.

# Case #2:  Legion of Decency (1934)

## Background

The setting was Washington, D.C. in April, 1933. Archbishop Amleto Cicognani, the newly arrived Apostolic Delegate [Representative of the Pope] to the United States, called for action to stem the increasing menace of the cinema. He deplored contemporary movies and claimed that the American church must assume a leadership role in cleaning up the films. According to Cicognani, the influence of Hollywood was felt around the world, and the movie industry was corrupting America and other nations with its portrayal of sex and violence.

The American Bishops met for their annual meeting the following November. A committee of bishops was appointed to do something about the motion picture situation, citing the speech by Cicognani the previous spring.

As the scenario unfolded within the US Catholic Church, a new movement was formed in early 1934 called the Legion of Decency. Though the Legion was to become a nation-wide organization, certain cities in the country, particularly those with large Catholic populations like Chicago, Philadelphia, New York, and Boston, became leaders in the campaign against indecent films.

The Motion Picture Code, written a few years earlier, was enforced for the first time in late 1934. The enforcement came, in part, from the pressure of the Legion of Decency (Moley). The Code was in effect, for all practical purposes, until the 1950's when Otto Preminger was the first to abandon it in making his film, *The Moon is Blue*.

## Problem

The issue facing Catholic leaders was how to make the Legion an effective tool against immoral motion pictures. The Legion, in turn, would clean up Hollywood and the world. This was a mission that the Catholic Church in the United States adopted. Boston, as a major Catholic metropolitan area, is a good representative city for looking at that work.

## Solution

In a letter dated May 10, 1934 to Cardinal William O'Connell, Archbishop of Boston, Archbishop John T. McNicholas who was the Chairman of the Episcopal Commission on Motion Pictures asked for the Cardinal's help "in furtherance of the campaign against indecent moving picture entertainment." In a letter that Cardinal O'Connell received from another bishop these words appear: "This letter is to inform you that we are undertaking a campaign against indecent shows." The action of the Church is called a *campaign*.

In an article that appeared in the Boston Archdiocesan Newspaper, *The Pilot,* on July 14, 1934, the word *crusade* appears. The front page story cited the Legion's efforts using these words: "Very many

Bishops have directed that the crusade against evil motion pictures be preached from every pulpit in their diocese, some stipulating that all pastors preach the crusade on a given Sunday, and others asking that it be emphasized several times."

Boston and the neighboring dioceses of Springfield and Fall River had 508 movie theaters. The Catholic population was over one million in Boston alone. There was considerable control over the attitudes and behavior of the faithful by Cardinal O'Connell and his representative, the local pastor of the individual parish.

With the scene consisting of the conflict between the permissiveness of the filmmakers and the desire to control moral behavior on the part of the local church, it seemed inevitable that the Bishop would call on the members of his diocese to do something about the terrible situation within the film industry. A controlling, powerful, hierarchial organization with strong moral influence, such as the Archdiocese of Boston, could effect change.

The actors in the Legion of Decency in Boston were stars, supporting players, and extras. Members of the group included the Pope, the Cardinal, local pastors, a representative of the Cardinal for the Legion who was Rev. Patrick Sullivan, S.J., a philosophy professor from Boston College, the city council, Catholic lay organizations, school children, and civic groups.

When Cardinal O'Connell addressed a group of Catholic women at the Boston Cathedral, he said, "Resolve not to visit the dens of vice—these gilded palaces of vice—which the theaters have become in this present day. How do you expect to keep the proper decent standards of women if you go to these picture houses where you see trash, vulgarity, and even worse."

Father Sullivan delivered an address to the Knights of Columbus' Annual Meeting in April, 1934. He charged that an educational medium such as motion pictures should be freed from immoral subjects tending to corrupt youth. The delegates adopted a resolution opposing the continued production of improper films, and planned to organize committees on this subject. A plan of action was to be placed before the Bishops for approval.

Local pastors made an announcement at Sunday Mass on July 22, 1934 about the Legion of Decency . Sacred Heart Parish in East Cambridge, MA had as its slogan that Sunday, "Take 'Sin' out of Cinema." The Church put pressure on local city officials. The Boston City Council passed this proposal at its July 23, 1934 meeting:

Resolved, that the City Council of Boston endorse the present campaign for purification of the Motion Picture Industry so that the citizens and especially the children of Boston may not have their minds contaminated by exhibition of salacious and vulgar motion pictures, and that the Mayor of Boston be requested to call a meeting of the Board of Censors with a view of banning from the theaters of Boston all objectionable motion pictures.

The Catholic weekly newspaper, *The Pilot*, ran articles in almost every edition in 1934 about the movement to clean up films. Catholic radio was also used to get the message out to devoted Catholics. The major secular Boston papers kept the city informed about the growth of the movement, especially when it was joined by other religious and civic organizations.

One pastor speaking on Sunday, July 22, 1934, at All Saints Parish in Roxbury, made this announcement: "A League of Decency has been formed in all the parishes of the Archdiocese to fight the evils of the Moving Picture Industry." A pledge to abide by the principles of the Legion was soon written and approved by the Bishops at their annual meeting in Washington, D.C. in 1935. Catholics recited the pledge every December well into the 1960's when a sexual revolution became the new scene in our country.

### Commentary

The results of the Legion of Decency campaign are documented by movie historian, Sklar (1975), who says,

In 1933-34, spurred by the changes in national mood brought about by the New Deal and prodded by the Legion of Decency, Hollywood directed its enormous powers of persuasion to preserving the basic moral, social, and economic tenets of traditional American culture.

To look at this campaign from the theoretical perspective of sociodrama, we have to begin by looking at who the actors were in the campaign. When the Catholic lay person or the local pastor spoke or wrote about the Legion, it was always in response to Bishops and the Pope, as well as all other Catholic leaders in the nation, who were behind the Legion. The control of those leaders over the lives of their followers surely had an influence over who became involved in the Legion. The Legion became important to people as they talked about how important it was to their religious leaders.

The words describing the Legion included *campaign*, *crusade*, *saving the morals of our children*, *communism*, *the Church*, and *sin*. These were the words used in radio addresses, speeches, sermons, letters, city council resolutions, and the secular press.

The effect of the Code's enforcement in the Fall of 1934 can be directly related to the powerful force of people interacting and identifying with this struggle for clean films *through language*. The Church gave people purpose and identity. They expressed their religious selves by becoming part of the language of battle and crusade against Hollywood. Good Catholics supported the Legion. Their identity as Catholics was tied up with their talk about the Legion as a Catholic entity. Indeed, the Legion was often referred to as the *Catholic* Legion.

Axiom #3 states:

> ***Social order is made possible precisely because we talk about it in certain ways, for certain purposes, in certain roles, in certain settings.***

This event was a massive public relations campaign, conducted with many of the principles of sociodrama. People wanted to influence the direction that Hollywood was taking and did so by calling upon the religious sentiment of American Catholics. That sentiment was expressed in the language of God, sin, church, morality, decency, and sex. The Church influenced its followers by calling upon them in the name of God and all that is decent. People responded in that setting because they wanted to be part of the Church. If they were not Catholic, they often responded because so many other non-Catholics were also saying "we've had enough."

## Case #3:  Abortion:  To Argue for the Same Cause

### *Background*

Since the Supreme Court ruled in 1973 that a woman could terminate her pregnancy in the first trimester, we have seen several groups emerge to either protest or defend that position. Each group has tried to influence public opinion. At the end of June, 1994, a Supreme Court decision ordered protestors to demonstrate quietly and keep at least 36 feet from a Florida abortion clinic. The ruling could effect more than 40 abortion clinics around the country which are currently under injunctions intended to provide relief from protests. Anti-abortion groups were angered by the ruling, while the head of the Feminist Majority called it a victory (Puga).

Three groups basically take the same pro-choice position on this issue, but argue for it from different world-views, or *different language*. Because sociodrama is a way of relating through the language that we use, this issue can be explored through a sociodrama lens.

The first group is the National Abortion Rights Action League (NARAL), which has tried to influence politicians to pass legislation that supports the 1973 Supreme Court decision. This case study will include the New Hampshire Chapter of NARAL which is located in Concord, New Hampshire. The second group is the Religious Coalition for Abortion Rights (NCAR), which has tried to influence religious leaders and those sympathetic to religion by saying abortion is a matter of religious freedom for a woman. The third group is Planned Parenthood which, from its start in the early part of this century, has promoted safe abortion if a woman so chooses. Plannned Parenthood's greatest influence has been through education. Planned Parenthood holds that all people, especially teenagers, need to know more about the responsibilities of family life, including contraception and abortion.

## Problem

The challenge facing each of these three groups was to convince their followers of one particular interpretation of the Supreme Court decision. Once their constituencies were aware of the group's interpretation and were supporting that interpretation, the next phase of activity was to attract more members to its cause, particularly those who would be willing to make a financial donation to support the work of the group.

## Solution

To look at the solution to the public relations portion of this issue, the language each group uses in its public relations literature must be reviewed.

## National Abortion Rights Action League (NARAL)

In their newsletter, the NARAL-NH (New Hampshire Chapter) group has targeted three pro-choice New Hampshire Senate candidates to receive extensive volunteer support from NARAL members in their general election campaigns. This is what we read in the newsletter:

Let's make sure we send solid, pro-choice legislators to Concord - check the election information contained in this Newsletter carefully, share it with your friends, and be sure to VOTE PRO-CHOICE ON NOVEMBER 4TH.

House-meetings are another strategy used to elicit new members. Here is another line from their newsletter:

House meetings are not a means to persuade anti-choice people to see the light! They are meant to mobilize and activate those people who are already pro-choice (and we are the majority, according to numerous public opinion polls.)

The anti-choice factions may be small in this state, but they devote much time, energy, and money to banning freedom of choice. They are fanatical and zealous and few people like their tactics; however, they have been successful in the past and will continue to exert political pressure on state legislators. We must be there to do the same for freedom of choice. We must be there for women's lives.

In a brochure, they say:

You know them as the 'Right to Life' people. They oppose abortion, but did you know...
The 'Right to Life' people are winning in their campaign to make your decision for you. And they won't stop without a fight. It's your choice. Keep it.

## Religious Coalition for Abortion Rights (RCAR)

The RCAR logo combines the religious symbols of the Cross (Christian) and the Menorah (Jewish). These symbols are intertwined to demonstrate the unity of purpose of the Religious Coalition for Abortion Rights members. In their brochure, they say:

Most Protestant and Jewish organizations believe there should be no abortion laws which reflect any one particular religious viewpoint. Rather, the state should remain neutral, leaving each faith free to practice and teach its beliefs as guaranteed by the United States Constitution.

The present attempts by an organized minority to overturn the Court's ruling are seen by these groups as a threat to the constitutional rights of women and to freedom of religion.

Through informational mailings and a monthly newsletter, RCAR stimulates citizen action by the members of religious communities who oppose any laws which would restrict the legal option of abortion.

A subgroup of the RCAR is the religiously-motivated pro-choice group called Catholics for a Free Choice. Their language sounds similar to the RCAR. Here are some words from their brochure:

We deplore the efforts of our hierarchy to impose through law its set of views on abortion on the US population. All Americans are free to follow their respective religious beliefs, guaranteed by the first Amendment to the Constitution. We especially reject the hierarchy's attempts to coerce the Catholic conscience and jeopardize the lives of Catholic women.

## Planned Parenthood

In the Planned Parenthood booklet, entitled *Nine Reasons Why Abortions are Legal*, we read:

At the most basic level, the abortion issue is not really about abortion. It is about the value of women in society.

The anti-abortion leaders really have a large purpose. They oppose most ideas and programs which can help women achieve equality and freedom.

The anti-abortion movement is increasingly hostile to the actual concerns of real people. They fail to acknowledge that lives are being ruined every day. Not by legal abortion, but by lack of education and access to contraception.

## Commentary

The language of the preceeding groups, as they make their argument in favor of abortion, must be reviewed. Sociodrama is concerned with the kinds of words used to enable both the organization and its audiences to feel a part of the drama. Axiom #1 of sociodrama states:

***Language is a way of explaining and a way of creating motives that lead to a certain kind of action.***

Language enables the actors to launch their drama in the public interest. Consider the language used in the following three groups' material:

## National Abortion Rights Action League (NARAL)

"We" share with friends that we are "in this fight together." In NARAL's newsletter, the editor and the reader are members of the same community of friends. If you take the NARAL position, you are a friend.

Taking a stand *against* abortion, as anti-choice people do, labels you a fanatic or an enemy. Clearly spelled out in the NARAL material is the line of battle drawn between the pro- and anti-choice factions.

## Religious Coalition for Abortion Rights (RCAR)

The symbol of a cross and a menorah shows a unity of religions on the abortion issue. To enjoy freedom of religion is to be American. Religious faiths have different views on abortion, but each should be allowed to practice its beliefs and not force them on others. As good followers, the Catholics for Free Choice (CFC) implore their hierarchy not to impose Catholic dogma on the rest of the country.

## Planned Parenthood

To be pro-abortion is to value women. Any ideas that can help liberate women ought to be encouraged. Abortion is one of those ideas. We also need sex education which includes material about contraception and abortion. Education will make us free.

Notice the language in each of these groups. They want us to identify with a cause and use words like equality, freedom, education, and religion to support a woman's right to have an abortion. They are arguing for the same position but from different directions by expressing themselves in different *language*. A question that might be raised, however, is that the same words — freedom, education, equality, and education — might be used by the opposing group as they make their case for preserving the life of the fetus.

What we see here is a need to make people feel part of a common drama by using words that enable them to become involved in the scene through identification as heroes or heroines who fight a common enemy. At the same time, the words used in the brochures and newsletters highlight the hierarchy that is present in our struggle for a certain social order (e.g. phrases like: We are more on target than the Right-to-Life group; We are the truth.). Axiom #7 states:

*In public relations we create sociodramas which have a certain built-in hierarchy and with which the organization and the public identify.*

Axiom #9 also helps explain the kind of language used by this group:

**We identify with victims, scapegoats, and stereotypes in interpreting the messages of public relations strategies and thus create images concerning the organization as it relates to us.**

With the abortion issue, which sets off a great deal of emotion in people, the sociodrama needs to be spelled out quite clearly because people do identify with one or the other drama. Axiom #10 explains it well:

*Communication, and public relations specifically, does not involve giving them a message, but instead identifies with others in a common drama.*

## Case #4:  Phillips Petroleum Takeover

### Background

In December, 1984, T. Boone Pickens, a Texas oil man, wanted to take over Phillips Petroleum in Bartlesville, Oklahoma.  He intended to buy out the company through the purchase of a majority of stock in the company. Bartlesville had been the home of Phillips Petroleum since 1917.  The company was not just a place to work. It was the largest employer in the town (8000 people work there out of a town population of 40,000)  and had done much to support the community over the years.

### Problem

Phillips was faced with the problem of negative public opinion from its employees and town leaders.  The town feared the loss of jobs if Phillips' corporate headquarters were moved, even though Pickens had said he would not move the company to Texas.  A campaign had to be launched that would change Pickens' takeover decision.  The people of Bartlesville had to rally around the company as its own. The focus of the campaign was that Bartlesville would fight the take-over.

## Solution

Several steps were taken by the town with the indirect involvement of Phillips Petroleum. A pep rally at the Bartlesville Community Center, called a "unity rally," was the first step. The rally, organized by the Chamber of Commerce, attracted over 3000 people and broke attendance records for events of a similar nature. Letters were written to the editor of the local paper to keep the company there. A float in the Christmas parade had a character called *Boone-Buster*, a takeoff from the *Ghostbusters* film.

A children's crusade was also begun. Teachers supported this movement. School children wrote letters to President Reagan about the hostile takeover and what Phillips meant to the town. The local churches also rallied to Phillips' side. Prayer vigils were held. When Boone reversed his decision, two days before Christmas, church leaders requested 60 seconds of silence at the annual Christmas service in thanksgiving for answered prayers.

A December 13, 1984 editorial in the *Enid Morning News* reads:

> The pirating of corporate structures is nothing new for Pickens and his partners.... As of this writing the takeover project is being slowed by litigation. Phillips officials are fighting back in the courts and although they are underdogs, most Oklahomans would like to see them win. No question - Phillips is better for the state and nation than Boone's Texas raiders who would take its place.

The MacNeil/Lehrer Newshour of December 13, 1984 said:

> Without official proclamation by the city's government, Phillips 66 officials received total and enthusiastic support from the public at last night's meeting in the packed community center that Phillips' donations helped build.

Rudy Taylor, publisher, is quoted at the rally as saying:

> You are our brothers and sisters and when Phillips Petroleum Company is attacked in any way, we feel that it's a slap in the face directly because without Phillips, we would just be *Mayberry RFD* mighty fast.

## Commentary

The press coverage was primarily in sympathy with the official position of Phillips. That the local and state media were clearly on the side of the company in this problem is born out in the kind of coverage the media allotted Phillips over a period of several weeks.

The town identified itself as a victim through its various groups: workers, families, business, politicians, school children, and even religious groups. The enemy clearly was Boone (e.g., the word "Boone-Buster" used in the Christmas float). Prayers were said to implore the divinity for help in this campaign, and at Christmas there was a moment of silence to thank God for delivery. The children were involved in a *crusade* through their letter- writing. They were fighting to save their town and way of life. Much drama through language was happening on several fronts in this town. Axiom #5:

*We relate to each other through written or spoken words that have the characteristics of drama.*

The Boone Pickens contingent, on the other hand, is called *pirates* and *raiders*. They are clearly the enemy. Phillips is depicted as struggling to deal with the problem and is deemed the *underdog* by the press. According to the local media and the townspeople, Phillips and Bartlesville are being victimized by Pickens. Clearly, the townspeople wanted victory in this campaign. Because of the language used in the campaign, the writers and speakers were able to build their support groups. They knew others would identify with them. Axiom #8 refers to how we use words actively:

*The recipients of the messages we create and send are active viewers, listeners, or readers.*

The events began on December 5. On December 24 Mr. Pickens said he would not buy out Phillips Petroleum. Within that three-week period enough public relations activity was generated to create an atmosphere in which Mr. Pickens felt that he could not proceed. It was a victory for the town.

# Case #5:  Midland College:  Images of a New Videoroom

## *Background*

Midland College is a small, private New England college with a student population of about 1,000. A new gameroom with about 15 video games was set up in the student center.

## *Problem*

The college administration, especially the student services department, felt that various groups within in the college (as well as people from the wider community) had not been using the gameroom enough. The town already had two of its own privately owned video parlors that were attracting young townspeople, as well as Midland students. The problem was getting more of the Midland community to use the college videoroom.

Student services personnel decided to undertake a promotional campaign.  Before the campaign was begun, however, it was decided to research the perception that people had of videogames in general and the gameroom in particular and use that research in the promotion. From that research they could create a campaign to increase public acceptance and minimize negative public opinion.  The motivation behind the research was to enable the public relations professional to have concrete data on which to base his/her public relations planning and writing.

## *Solution*

The process used to research the images was twofold:  focus interviews and Q sorting methodology.  These are the methods discussed in Chapter 5 and are an important vehicle for applying the theory of sociodrama to public relations practice. They help get in touch with subjective meanings or images held by the audience.

## Focus Interviews

A focus group interview was conducted with ten students who are regular users of the gameroom. The questions used for the interviews were based on the five elements and the three levels of the drama in the sociodrama grid.

## Q sorting Methodology

A Q sort was then used.  A group of other students, faculty, and staff sorted a series of 48 short statements about videogames and the gameroom. The statements represented the dominant themes of the focus interviews and were chosen in such a way that each of the statements related to one of the 5 elements and to one of the 3 levels of the drama as closely as possible. The phrasing of each statement came directly from the interviews. The subjects were asked to sort the statements, on separate cards, according to this condition of instruction:

SORT THESE AS THEY REPRESENT HOW YOU FEEL ABOUT VIDEOGAMES AND OUR GAMEROOM.

## Results

Twelve Q sorts were usable from the ones administered to the representative groups. Table 1 shows how the subjects factored. The factors are generated by using the correlations that are created by the subjects' scores. From Table 1 you can see that three factors were derived with the following number of subjects factoring on each of them: 2 on Factor 1, 5 on Factor 2, and 2 on Factor 3. Subjects 2, 3 and 9 did not factor out significantly on a single factor.

The three factors create what one might refer to as the *Images of the Gameroom*. Three images are distinguished from what people say about the gameroom. Each image emerges with its own individual characteristics.

Factor 1, or Image 1, is the **Challenge** image. The statements that scored the highest and are the most positive on this factor are:

36.  Some places have five games for a dollar, which is nice. I would rather spend a dollar than a couple of quarters here or there.

39.  There ought to be more tournaments.

37.  I like playing in the dark with just music.

And these subjects feel most negative about these statements:

45.  The gameroom atmosphere is bad. It's just a room with machines.

14.  It's better to have video games and people socializing than seeing students in their rooms drinking.

## Table 1

Factor Loadings

| Subject | Factor 1 | Factor 2 | Factor 3 |
|:---:|:---:|:---:|:---:|
| 1. | -.034 | .624 | -.197 |
| 2. | .564 | .439 | .067 |
| 3. | .062 | .376 | .443 |
| 4. | .729 | .20 | .043 |
| 5. | -.0 | .349 | -.045 |
| 6. | .015 | .019 | .342 |
| 7. | -.0 | .361 | .182 |
| 8. | .247 | -.08 | .672 |
| 9. | .61 | .00 | .369 |
| 10. | -.039 | .354 | -.321 |
| 11. | .147 | .599 | .203 |
| 12. | .351 | -.282 | -.142 |

These subjects, all students who use the gameroom, consider video games a challenge. They would like tournaments and are generally more concerned with the games than improving the atmosphere. If people want to drink, that's all right, just as it's all right for them to indulge in video games. They don't see games as a substitute for drinking. The image these subjects construct by their statements is that of a challenging atmosphere. The staff might provide even greater challenge if they offered video game tournaments.

The second image or Factor 2 could be called the **Wasteful** image. This group, made up primarily of students and a few staff, are critical of video games in general and the gameroom in particular. Very few have played the games. This group is most positive about these statements:

18.    I think video games are a waste of money.

16.     A lot of people who were not brought up on video games
        think they are bad.

21.     People are competitive in video games. They compete
        against themselves and their friends.

They suggest that video games are a waste of money, but also nurture a competitive spirit in the players. On both of these issues they are critical. They also indicate an opinion that unless you were brought up on video game-playing, you think negatively about it. They also feel strongly about this statement:

24.     Sometimes you find yourself talking about games outside
        the gameroom and you realize how stupid the whole thing
        is.

When they play games and talk about it they feel uncomfortable with themselves, which again indicates that they do not like the game or playing the game. They project their discussion of this issue on others as well as themselves. Because they don't like them, others ought to feel the same way. As a result, they justify their behavior by projecting it onto others. The **Wasteful** image feels most negative about these statements:

9.      We are expected, as a College, to have video games.
2.      They are better than going to the Pub.
31.     When I'm frustrated, I'll just drop in there.

This Image does not feel that the college must keep up with the current video game trend. It is important to relieve frustration, but this group prefers the local bar to the gameroom. They seem to want to relieve their tension with a drink and want others to do the same. At the very least, they do not want people relieving tension by playing video games. And finally, they feel negative about this statement:

11.     Faculty are scared to go into the gameroom.

Though there are no faculty in this Factor, some of the subjects themselves use the gameroom, so they don't think faculty would be afraid to use it even though they think that people not brought up on the games have negative views of them (Statement 16).

The subjects think video games are a waste and they, for the most part, do not play the games. This group reflects its own feelings by the way they have constructed their Image. This Image flows from and through their talk about their behavior. Their talk reflects their behavior and constructs an image that video games are a waste of time, money, and energy.

The third image, or Factor 3, is **Relaxation**. This group, made up of one staff member and one faculty member, see the gameroom and video games as an opportunity to relax. The statements they feel most positive about are:

19.  Video games can be relaxing.
3.   I use the games more as a break.
10.  The hours that the gameroom is open are good.
8.   The student that comes to Midland is used to having this kind of recreational activity.
38.  The gameroom is good because all college students are there.

The staff member uses the gameroom frequently, but the faculty member does not use it at all. Both, however, feel quite positive about the games. They say, in fact, that it is *good* to have a gameroom for students. They seem to project their appreciation of video games and the gameroom onto students. They feel that one can get a sense of relaxation from the gameroom. The statements this group feels most negative about are:

1.   Video games are a good excuse not to do something.
12.  Older people who didn't grow up with video games tend to see them as evil.
34.  I would just as soon walk downtown than wait to play a video game.

They like video games. As "older people," they feel that they (i.e. older people who didn't grow up on games) can enjoy them and have some fun with them. Again they seem to project their own Image of the games and the gameroom on others.

A different drama is enacted by the subjects in each of the Images. In the first Image, **Challenge**, the emphasis is on the Scene. The statements that are most important to this Factor are all from the Scene as one element of the Grid. They simply like to play the game and do play regularly. They like the fact that the place exists and are not particularly concerned about any negative features.

In the second Image, **Wasteful**, the emphasis from the selection of significant statements is on the Act. They simply do not like the *act* of video games in any way. Most do not play. Those who do play do not use the gameroom very much. Particulars about video games or the gameroom are not important in this image. This group simply does not see any value in playing video games and forms their view of the games and the gameroom in that light.

The third Image, **Relaxation**, emphasizes the behind-the-scenes and on-stage levels of the drama. They find what's being done in the gameroom by the staff to be quite adequate. They also feel that the games in themselves are a fine form of relaxation. It is interesting to note that the member of the staff who is on this factor is also directly responsible for the gameroom and its operation. He projects a favorable image on the gameroom, perhaps, because that's his job and he likes it!

What we notice, therefore, in all three images is that the subjects enact a different drama by the way they talk about their image of the games and, in that way, construct their image.

## Conclusion

Three images of the gameroom were constructed by the subjects. If behavior follows the image, we can say that the image will be the way various groups in the college act in regard to video games and the gameroom. It is not evident from this research that students think in one way, faculty in another, and staff in a third. The perception of the three groups has to do with their *involvement* with video games and, in turn, their involvement in the game is directly related to their image of the games.

The behavior of the audiences within the college community will flow from these images. In other words, those who relate to the **Challenge** image will act out that image regarding the gameroom. The **Wasteful** image not only reflects but guides the behavior of those people who view the concept of video games negatively. And finally, those who project a **Relaxation** image will see the gameroom in that light. Such is the sensitivity of the Q sort research methodology. Its power rests on the concept that people make sense of their worlds from a subjective view of themselves and their own needs.

## Commentary

A promotional plan for the gameroom is now possible because we know how the various audiences perceive video games and what their images of this particular gameroom are. Axiom #1 says:

> ***Language is a way of explaining and a way of creating motives that lead to a certain kind of action.***

The way people talk about the matter is the way they relate to it. We don't simply *use* words. Words are our link to the world and our source of identification with ourselves and with one another. Axiom #3:

> ***Social order is made possible precisely because we talk about it in certain ways, for certain purposes, in certain roles, in certain settings.***

The participants in the research talk about how they understand videogames and the Midland gameroom. Through that discussion they got in touch with their own drama in regard to the issue — a scene they liked or didn't like, serving a certain purpose, certain kinds of characters that hang around there, talking in a certain way, and finally offering them an enjoyable experience or something they avoid like the plague. There is no right or wrong here. There is simply the perception of the matter at hand. That perception or image is what sociodrama is all about.

It is the same for those who did the Q-sorting. Through their sorting, the subjects understood their own feelings, opinions, and ideas about videogames by becoming involved in the conversation about them. As participants, they heard themselves reflect on the statements and began to understand how they felt about the issue. They got in touch with their subjective world.

Language is a way of becoming part of something bigger than ourselves. That language, expressed in dramatic metaphors, is our path to involvement with others concerning a certain issue, in many different kinds of ways: joy, love, anger, hate. Sociodrama points out that link in Axiom #5:

> ***We relate to each other through written or spoken words that have the characteristics of drama.***

The college administration proceeded to embark on a campaign based on these images of the gameroom. Radio spots, newspaper stories, and posters were the principal media used.

# Case #6: ABC Technics Co. in Culver, Massachusetts

## *Background*

ABC Technics located a new facility in Culver, Massachusetts, in the heart of the high-tech area, and needed some information to begin communication planning. What perceptions or *image* did the outside public have of them? With what is learned about an issue from the public a communication plan can be created to reinforce positive opinions and change negative or unacceptable opinions. ABC Technics would operate, therefore, using a proactive model of communication: preparing communication to speak to an audience as they *are* rather than simply preparing material for them based on what the company thinks the public perception might be. The company would be more effective with its communication by using such a proactive strategy.

Primary ssumptions behind the research were discussed at an early meeting with ABC Technics Communication representatives. These assumptions were used in the design of the research phase and were implicitly being tested throughout the project.

The theory or background for the study was sociodrama. Audiences act toward an organization, not as it *is* but as they perceive or image it. The source for our images are the people that we talk to on a regular basis: family, friends, neighbors, as well as other opinion sources. By voicing our opinion or feelings about an organization, we construct our image of it. That image, in turn, provides the motivation for the way in which we act toward the organization.

## *Problem*

The research problem was to understand the community perceptions of the ABC Technics facility. The audiences were defined as local residents, city officials, business leaders, media representatives, and other opinion leaders.

## *Solution*

The primary method for this research project was providing the subjects an opportunity to talk about their images or perceptions of the company. Both focus groups and Q sort methodologies were used.

Four images or factors were produced by the subjects.

**A.**   **Diversified Image**
This group of businesses, educators, and city officials, looked upon ABC Technics as adding diversification to the city.

**B.**   **Improving Image**
This image indicated that the financial picture of Culver improved with the arrival of ABC: increased income from rental property and their new facility was an attractive building.

**C.**   **Unknown Image**
This image was held predominantly by the media. ABC was not known by the local community.

**D.**   **Fearful Image**
This image was created by other members of the media who felt ABC presented a danger to the community be cause of dangerous chemicals that could be used at the plant.

## *Commentary*

Sociodrama is the basis for the process of understanding what images people had of ABC. The crucial component of the research process was to allow representative subjects to talk about the company. It then became the responsibility of ABC's communication strategist to create messages in appropriate media forms that responded to the perceptions of the public.

## Case #7: Images of Girl Scout Leaders

### *Background*

The Swift Water Girl Scout Council is located in Manchester, New Hampshire. The Council wanted to embark on a new leadership recruitment campaign and needed to communicate with potential leaders in the community. Before an extensive campaign was undertaken, it was important to know what images of a typical Girl Scout Leader were out there.

If the prevailing image of Girl Scout leaders or leadership was

Figure 1

## SOCIODRAMA GRID

[The numbers in the cells represent the short statements which were derived from the interviews with the representative subjects.]

*Levels of the Drama*

| *Elements of the Drama* | a. Behind the scene | b. On Stage | c. Outside the Theater |
|---|---|---|---|
| 1. act | 2, 10, 24, 28 | 7, 8, 44 | 16, 21, 45 |
| 2. scene | 1, 26, 34 | 9, 22, 29 | 20, 25, 36 |
| 3. means | 3, 11, 32 | 19, 23, 27 | 17, 18, 38, 46 |
| 4. actors | 14, 33, 41 | 6, 13, 15 | 30, 37, 39, 40 |
| 5. purpose | 4, 5, 42 | 43, 47, 48 | 12, 31, 3 |

negative, the Council could design communication strategy to change the opinion. On the other hand, if the images seem to mirror the goals of the Council, the subsequent communication effort could be to continue the message in its existing form to that audience. In any event, planned communication in response to images that the audience holds is one major step toward achieving organizational objectives.

## Problem

The research question was:

> We will try to understand the images of present leaders concerning what Girl Scouting means to them and what their role is in that process.

Sociodrama says that the leaders have images about what happens behind the scenes, images of how scouting relates directly to them, and images how others in the community view a Girl Scout Leader. These images guide their behavior.

## *Solution*

It was decided that for this project, the present Girl Scout leaders would be the subject of the research. In that way, their perceptions of their role and their motivation for assuming that role could be better understood and used to attract others to the same job. Two focus groups were conducted with 18 leaders. The groups represented different ages and included both married and single members. The interview questions were based on the five elements and the three levels of the sociodrama grid.

About 72 statements were generated from the focus interviews. These statements were expressions of feelings, opinions, and attitudes. Forty-eight (48) short statements were chosen and divided into the various levels and elements of the sociodrama Grid within the 15 cells (see Figure 1).

The Q sort portion of the project was mailed to 100 other troop leaders who again represented different ages and marital status. This group was generated from a random sampling of troop leaders within the Swift Water Girl Scout Council area. They were not the same subjects who were interviewed in the focus group portion of the project. The subjects were asked to mail the responses directly to the researcher and 31% did so.

The subjects were asked to sort a series of statements with the following condition of instruction:

SORT THESE AS THEY REFLECT YOUR FEELINGS
AND ATTITUDES ABOUT BEING A GIRL SCOUT LEADER.

Three factors or images emerged from the sorting. Though they all talked about *scouting* and *what it means to be a Leader*, the leaders did not all see the same thing. There were three different images or ways of looking at leadership.

The first image was the **Personal Enrichment** Image. Look at which statements were most important to this group:

47.   Being a Leader is a learning experience. You learn a lot.

43.   I've learned a lot as a leader, especially how to deal with people.

4.    A leader has as much fun as the children do.

This group valued the experience of being a leader. That was the most important thing to them. They certainly also saw their role as a leader as important. They felt quite strongly about this statement:

42.   You make a difference. You touched someone's life. What a reward for being a leader.

Notice in that statement that the leader clearly affirmed getting something out of the experience. This goes along with their image of personal enrichment. A look at what was negative in the statements for this group found the following:

24.   The training is overwhelming to some new leaders. This scares them.

This image viewed the training as an opportunity for personal growth. They had no negative feelings about that kind of experience. Then, as if to challenge the Council, troop leaders rejected this statement strongly:

41.   If you are always looking for leaders, you are going to be frustrated.

For this group, troop leadership is an opportunity for people to grow as people. People are looking for this kind of chance, so in no way is it frustrating to look for leaders. People want to grow and the Girl Scout organization provides the challenge and the opportunity.

The subjects in this group were from both large and small towns. Their age group was primarily 30-39, and all were female. The drama that this group enacted for their image was *purpose*. Most of their statements were from this area in the sociodrama grid. That means their image of scouting was centered on *why* they were doing it. In this case, it was clearly for personal enrichment. They were not hesitant to declare that motivation.

The second image, **Supportive Environment**, is quite different from the first. Here are the statements that are most important to this group:

22. New leaders need help especially the first year which is the hardest.
34. The Office fails because they do not go out and see the local problems that might exist. As troops drop down, they need to look into this.
14. Knowing that a leader has support for her role from the organization is important.

In all these statements, the group felt that leading a troop means acting in a supportive environment. They did not hesitate to criticize the Council Office when necessary, as having support from the main office was critical for this group. The statements that were most negative were the following:

10. Some of the leaders feel that if they ask for help from parents they are failing.
37. No parents want to get involved.

In keeping with the **Supportive Environment** Image this group did not hesitate to ask parents for help. In fact, they denied that parents do not want to get involved. This group surely saw the benefit of Girl Scouting (high positive response to Statement #42), but they linked that value with getting support on a regular basis from several sources.

The image of scouting for them and their role focused on the drama *behind the scenes*, where most of their statements originated. *Behind the scenes* can be equated with getting the necessary support to do the job.

The third image was the **Service** Image. The statements that were most important were:

42. You make a difference. You touched someone's life. What a reward for being a Leader.
13. I would tell mothers who might be Leaders: Schools today teach competition. Girl Scouts help the child learn to work in a group. In Girl Scouts the girl dares to fail.

Leading a troop is doing a service for the community. Leaders help the girl develop skills not learned in school. The statement they felt most negatively about was:

> 3.      It is difficult to say anything tangible about being a leader. You can't sell that to future leaders.

They felt that it is important to attract new leaders and something "tangible" like "we do a significant community service" could indeed be said.

The members who formed this image enacted a drama *on stage*. They tended to see the importance of Scout leadership as serving their community. They felt a part of that community through their involvement as Scout Leaders.

In summing up, three images of the Girl Scout Leader role can be identified:

1.      Personal Enrichment
2.      Supportive Environment
3.      Service

## Commentary

The images of the Girl Scout Leader were created by the subjects as they interacted with one another, both in the focus groups and in the sorting. The subjects were representative of the Council's leaders in terms of demographics. If every leader in the Council had been involved in either a focus group or the Q-sorting, the project would probably have arrived at similar results.

If, as Boulding (1956) pointed out, behavior follows from the image, we can say that the image is the way the various leaders in the Council act in regard to both the Council and their role as troop leaders. They feel positively or negatively about that role based on the image they have of Scout leadership in general.

The concept of image is connected with the *drama of communication* or how people play different roles, with various means, in a particular scene, in a definite form of action, for a certain purpose. The subjects have images that involve all of these elements and are not simply passive onlookers. They construct their own drama and build an image by interacting with themselves and others through discussion at the focus group sessions and through sorting the statements.

The image that a particular leader holds of troop leadership supports her own ego-involvement. In other words, those who hold the image of leadership as **Personal Enrichment** see scouting leadership as an opportunity for growth in their own personal lives. Those who see leadership as a **Supportive Environment** may not support or even understand the **Personal Enrichment** image. All they see is that they need the support of others to do their job: the Council office, other leaders, and parents.

What assists our view of life is the way we define things and act toward them. We make judgements, form opinions, express feelings, and let others know what we like or don't like because it either helps or threatens us. Such behavior is neither good nor bad. It is simply the way we act to make sense of things and at the same time defend our way of looking at the world.

One person's behavior in the role of a Girl Scout leader flows from the perceptions of that particular leader. People do not see the same *leadership*. They see what supports their view of themselves and their own needs. Those who need personal enrichment see leadership as an opportunity for fulfilling that need. Those who see it as **Service**, see troop leadership as a way of giving to the community.

This research means that the Council's communication planning can now recognize the different images and respond to the images in a campaign. For example, those people we want to recruit who hold the image of **Personal Enrichment** will need to hear and see that leading a Girl Scout troop is an opportunity to develop skills and strengths for personal fulfillment. The same approach will have to be taken with the other two images.

Creating a mosaic out of the images of the Girl Scout Leader shows three separate areas (see Figure 2). Each of the areas or Images expresses a different color or nuance for the Council. Potential leaders, as well as the actual leaders, will relate to one or another of those images. Each leader could be mapped on the mosaic and see where she/he feels most comfortable in regard to the leadership role. Individual leaders might feel that one of the Images represents them better than another, or that a couple of them fit quite well since they can identify with both.

The Council produced an outstanding slide presentation which employed all three images. This was the major media form and was used extensively throughout the year.

Figure 2

Images of Girl Scout Leadership: A Mosaic

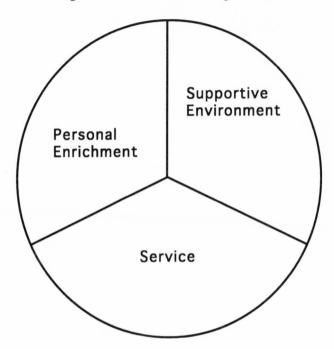

## References

Boulding, K.E. (1956). *The Image: Knowledge in life and society.* Ann Arbor:
    University of Michigan Press.
Moley, R. (1945). *The Hays office.* New York: Bobbs-Merrill Co.
Puga, A. (1994) Court ok's limits on abortion protestors. *Boston Globe*, July 1, p. 1,6.
Sklar, R. (1975). *Movie-made America: A social history of American movies.*
    New York: Random House.
Zemke, R. (1987). *Contact! Training employees to meet the public.* Training. pp. 41-45.

# Chapter 7

# Theory Application and Exercises

## Introduction

Someone once said, "If you fail to plan, plan to fail." That statement certainly highlights the need to take planning seriously. A public relations practitioner has to be able to plan, and this chapter will introduce the reader to public relations planning using sociodrama. Here the reader will have a chance to practice public relations planning through a series of exercises, using the Public Relations Planning Guide in Figure 1.

So far this book has been a discussion of public relations theory. The question the reader must now face is: How do I apply this theory to my own work? This chapter provides the tools to apply sociodrama in the workplace.

Take the exercises seriously. They are all cases that present a real public relations problem. Each organization needs professional help with a particular situation or event. You should treat each scenario as if you were the professional hired to facilitate a solution.

Below you will see a planning guide. Draw or trace the guide on a separate piece of paper as you work on each individual case. Try to address as many of the six categories as possible and be as precise as you can.

The items on the planning guide are OBJECTIVE, TARGET PUBLIC, MEDIA FORM, MESSAGE, TIMING, and COST. Here are the definitions for each of these terms.

### Objective
What is the purpose of the particular public relations activity you are proposing? Ordinarily the action ought to be either to inform or to change behavior in some way, i.e. to enable people to buy, to vote, or to call. Be sure that you understand the public relations problem and that you can state it in your own words.

**Target Audience**

Which group or groups are you most interested in reaching? Be as specific as possible once you have analyzed the problem. They ought to be people that you can target rather than the *general public*, who are often impossible or difficult to reach. There are specific actors who are involved in the drama of your organization whether they are internal or external audiences.

**Media Form**

Choose any media form you think will be effective in achieving your public relations objective. The media form could be print, broadcast, cable; controlled or uncontrolled; interpersonal networking such as meetings aor conferences; group or organizational. Be sure you can defend your choice. Don't forget the local media.

**Message**

Be specific in the message you want to give. Be short and brief since you can expand the copy as you prepare it. Your words are important as a way of involving your audience to respond to the situation as outlined. Your target audience needs to identify with the words you choose.

**Timing**

What is your schedule for researching and preparing the message? When do you want to send it out? When do you want it to appear in the media? For the sake of this exercise, it might be sufficient if in an individual case you simply suggest Week 1, Week 2, Week 3, rather than a particular calendar date. Let each individual case be your guide.

**Cost**

For the sake of preparing a budget, it is important to know how much an individual public relations activity will cost the client or company. Be as close as possible to actual costs.

It is important that you look for sociodrama present in the action between the organization and its audiences. In stating your objective, you might address what you found out in your research about the image of the audiences or the organization.

Remember, the *words* of the campaign need to express involvement

Figure 1

Planning Guide

| Objective | Target Audience | Media Form | Message | Timing | Cost |
|---|---|---|---|---|---|
| | | | | | |

and identification with the organization and with one another. Images are presented in and through the language people use to talk about the organization, and the more down to earth and less abstract the language is, the better chance we have of being understood and finding identification with others.

Your task is to prepare a public relations plan for each of the following cases. Write the plan down and let your boss, your instructor, or your fellow classmates comment on it. Be as thorough as you can. The best public relations plan is one that is written by one individual and not a committee. That individual can, therefore, make any defense necessary for any part of the plan.

It is important to do one exercise at a time. Others you may work with in the implementation phase of the plan need to be able to comment on your plan. Their language can become another useful tool in preparing the message for your target audience. In sociodrama we know that we understand something in the way we talk about it. Getting in touch with the language people use about a subject or issue shows that you understand how to prepare a public relations plan to reach that audience.

Each exercise will have two sections:

1. Background
2. Problem

Your job is to complete the third portion of the case study, called "Solution."

Good Luck!

## Exercise 1: Buy Now, Study Later!

### *Background*

The President's administration has drastically slashed federal money for loans and scholarships for college tuition. The new tax reform law is expected to put a crimp in charitable contributions to academia and the aging of the baby boom generation portends significantly declining enrollments in coming years.

The state of Michigan approved a part layaway—part mutual fund program to help parents save for their children's college tuition. The program offers parents steep tuition discounts if they contribute over several years to the plan.

The Michigan State Treasurer, chief architect of the state's program says, "Our mission is to provide families not only with a guarantee of tuition, but peace of mind. Parents will no longer have to say, 'How are we going to pay for this kid to go to college?' as their children are growing up."

Michigan believes that it will achieve flexibility through such a plan. Not only can participants use their tuition guarantees at any of the state's 15 public universities and 29 community colleges, but they can also tap the program to cover at least part of tuition costs at out-of-state or private schools if they opt not to enter the Michigan system.

Though precise rates have yet to be determined, state officials estimate an investment of as little as $2500 on behalf of an infant born today could buy four years of tuition that might cost nearly $25,000 or more when the child reaches college age in 2012. Parents short of cash will be offered the chance to finance the tuition much like they would a car, paying through an installment plan or payroll deductions.

Revenues from the sale of tuition guarantees will be deposited in a large, state-administered mutual fund which will then be tapped to cover tuition payments for participants. Michigan's students must still meet academic requirements to get into college, although the state will refund slightly more than the original investment if a child does not go to college. Even in the event of an unfavorable IRS ruling, the state treasurer is confident that not only can he get lawmakers to give him a new go-ahead for the program but that Michigan parents will still enthusiastically come up with the cash to buy into it.

### Problem

You serve as public relations counsel to the state treasurer. Advise him as to how to win public support for this program. If people are not in favor of it, it will not last very long. If lawmakers are not in favor of it, it will not continue.

### Solution
What is your PR plan?

## Exercise 2: Limosine Service

### Background
Top Brass Limousine Service, located in the state capital of 30,000 people, is three months old. It has one competitor. The owner is happy that all the bills have been paid to date but would like to increase community awareness of his business. The service offers first-class chauffeured limousines that will take a customer "anywhere the roads go." Top Brass offers extras, like roses for the passengers, and the drivers wear tuxedos. An important facet of Top Brass' service is taking passengers to the international airport in a large, nearby city about 70 miles away. That service comprises about 75% of their business.

Top Brass has its office in a Main Street storefront. Their major clients are a few large businesses in the city. Their rates are $75.00 for the first hour and $20.00 for every hour thereafter. The company has three employees: the owner, her husband, and their son.

### Problem

How could public relations help this new company? Top Brass needs greater recognition and increased use of its services. You are one of the three employees of the company. In addition to driving limos as needed, you are also responsible for this organization's public relations.

### Solution

You want to create a public relations plan for Top Brass. Remembering that the company is new, you might suggest a plan for the coming year and then a long-range plan, which will guide the organization for the next five years.

## Exercise 3: Citizens Speak

### Background

You are the public relations director for a local chapter of Citizens Against Hand Guns. The objective of your organization is to get legislation passed that will outlaw handgun sales, thus helping to curb the violence that is increasing in our communities. You have discovered that your city (population 100,000) is the location of a new business, Worldwide Ammo, Inc. Worldwide Ammo is believed to be the first mail order ammunition company selling directly to the general public. There has been much public reaction against the company by critics who say it gives terrorists and criminals easy access to ammunition.

Since Congress approved mail order ammunition in November of 1986, World Ammo has been filling an average 200 orders a day, according to the owner. People across the country can pick up the telephone and dial 1-800-555-BANG to place an order. Before November 15th, only licensed dealers could buy ammunition via mail order. On November 15th, Congress changed the Federal Gun Control Act of 1968 to allow customers to receive ammunition through commercial delivery, not the U.S. Postal Service.

### Problem

As the public relations director of Citizens Against Hand Guns, it is your responsibility is to increase public support for gun control. Certainly the presence of Worldwide Ammo in your own city is something about which you must make a statement. You can use this concrete example to alert the public to the problems involved in making guns even more readily available.

World Ammo is new. Perhaps through your efforts the town will exert pressure on the business. Perhaps local and state legislators will have to be drafted to support your public relations campaign. Your task is to mount a public relations campaign against the company.

### Solution

You must first win support for your plan from the executive director and the board of directors of your organization. Your plan must address the goals of your organization in terms of the problem with Worldwide Ammo, Inc.

## Exercise 4: Wang Leaves Town

### Background

Holyoke, Massachussets is a town of 44,678 people, located in the central part of the state. It is about 80 miles west of Boston, directly north of Hartford, Connecticut and thus a link to New York City from the Northeast.

Wang, one of the largest computer companies in the East, built a facility in Holyoke with a $2-million contribution from the city. The company recently decided, however, to close the Holyoke plant. In six months, Wang will be leaving Holyoke and 160 people will be out of work. Mayor Ernest E. Proulx says that the company which bought the plant and 180 surrounding acres, Monarch Capital Corporation, promises comparable growth to what Wang enjoyed. Monarch is the 135th largest company in the world. Monarch President, Gordon N. Oakes, Jr., says his company and Wang hope to retain some of the laid-off workers for data-processing jobs at the two insurance subsidiaries that will be housed at the plant.

Oakes says Monarch chose the spot because of its nearness to Interstate 91 and the Massachusetts Turnpike and because of the land which came with the building. He says the company will study the land with an eye to further development.

### Problem

You are the public relations director for Wang at its Holyoke plant. You will be moving to Wang Corporate Headquarters in Lowell, Massachusetts (about 70 miles away) and so you have a job when this is over. Wang has to convince its workers that the move is necessary. The town also must continue to hold a good opinion of Wang. How can this be done smoothly when so many people are going to be affected by the move?

### Solution
You need to devise a public relations plan for the next six months to help ease the transition. You want to continue to support both Wang and the town in the move.

## Exercise 5:  Gourmet Chocolates

### Background
Antron's is a gourmet food store in a town of 30,000. It is the only store that specializes in high quality food, including gourmet chocolates. Antron's has been open about a year and offers a bakery, packaged foods, and take-out. Business is very good. Annual per capita consumption of chocolate in the United States grew from 8.5 pounds in 1980 to 11.2 pounds in 1985, while total sales grew from $3.1 billion to $4.8 billion. "People are eating more healthfully; they're exercising more; they're drinking less," says Barbara Albright, editor-in-chief of *Chocolatier Magazine.* "When it comes to dessert, this is the time to treat themselves, and when they splurge, they want it to be the highest quality, richest thing they can splurge on."

The premium-chocolate business has followed in the footsteps of designer ice cream, gourmet chocolate chip cookies, and other specialty foods as they've gone into wider distribution. People are becoming more interested in the way things taste and are becoming more quality-conscious about food.

The lure of higher margins for premium chocolates has attracted large chocolate manufacturers, as well as specialty retailers and entrepreneurs, and has heated up competition considerably. "There are Americans around the country standing in line for truffles at $25.00 a pound. That's something five years ago that would have been impossible to predict," says Carmen Dubroc, vice president for marketing for Godiva Chocolatier, an 80-year old Belgian chocolate maker that was acquired by the Campbell Soup Company in the late 1960's.

## Problem

Antron's offers a wide selection of gourmet chocolates and would like people to know that in hopes that they will make their chocolate purchases at Antron's. The store does a good business on holidays like Valentine's Day, but would like to keep the chocolate business strong all year.

You are a public relations counsultant. Antron's has hired you to increase chocolate awareness in the town, and to spread the word that Antron's is the place to buy that chocolate.

## Solution

Create a public relations plan for the next 12 months that you can propose to the store.

# Exercise 6: 800 Directory

## Background

About 20 years ago, Paul Montana of Claverack, New York, put together the first 800 directory. His first result was a book containing about 2,600 toll-free 800 numbers. It sold for $2.00. This year's edition, with 43,000 numbers, sells for $17.95. Businesses throughout the nation are included. Customers or clients like to call a company without charge so there is a wide use of the 800 numbers across the nation. Frequently, however, you cannot use an 800 number to call a business in your own state. To order a copy you just have to call 1-800-447-4700.

## Problem

The directory, called the Toll Free Digest, is not very well known around the country. The company would like to increase national awareness of the digest in order to increase sales this year. You are the public relations director for the Toll Free Digest Company. You are to design a six month public relations campaign to publicize the digest throughout the United States.

## Solution

Decide on who would be a possible market for this directory: businesses, consumers, government, etc. Then proceed to prepare a plan that will reach them in a way that will produce some action in favor of the Digest.

# Appendix:
# The Ten Axioms of Sociodrama

1. Language is a way of explaining and a way of creating motives that lead to a certain kind of action.

2. Sociodrama is not concerned with only content or agency in communication but how people use the words to define themselves.

3. Social order is made possible precisely because we talk about it in certain ways, for certain purposes, in certain roles, in certain settings.

4. Sociodrama is not concerned with how society persuades us, but how words about society persuade us to act in certain ways in our social relationships.

5. We relate to each other through written or spoken words that have the characteristics of drama.

6. Social interaction is not a process, but a dramatic expression, an enactment of roles by individuals who seek to identify with each other in their search to create social order.

7. In public relations we create sociodramas which have a certain built-in hierarchy and with which the organization and the public identify.

8. The recipients of the messages we create and send are active viewers, listeners, or readers.

9. We identify with victims, scapegoats, and stereotypes in interpreting the messages of public relations strategies and thus create images concerning the organization as it relates to us.

10. Communication, and public relations specifically, does not involve giving someone a message, but instead identifies with others in a common drama.

These axioms are adapted from the work of Hugh Dalziel Duncan (1909-1970).